A Memoir in C-Minor

by

Agnes Karpathi

DORRANCE PUBLISHING CO., INC.
PITTSBURGH, PENNSYLVANIA 15222

All Rights Reserved
Copyright © 2010 by Agnes Karpathi
No part of this book may be reproduced or transmitted
in any form or by any means, electronic or mechanical,
including photocopying, recording, or by any information
storage and retrieval system without permission in
writing from the author.

ISBN: 978-1-4349-0492-8
Printed in the United States of America

First Printing

For information or to order additional books, please write:
Dorrance Publishing Co., Inc.
701 Smithfield St.
Pittsburgh, Pennsylvania 15222
U.S.A.
1-800-788-7654
www.dorrancebookstore.com

Alexander Zinoviev: "My soul is my fortress."

FOREWORD

A lifetime has gone by since the events related in these pages. I became a grandma. My life took on normal regularity and no one suspected what was behind me, unless I chose to speak about it. For many years I didn't bring it up. I lived for my family and in turn they made me happy. My children are real Americans and my whole life changed to such extent that I often wonder if those things really happened. Of course I know better; I cannot and do not want to blot out the past. I merely buried it in my younger years in an effort to live normally within a happy family frame. But now that there is only a little time left for me, I wanted to jot down on paper some of those events that formed my life and affected it.

I started out with the beautiful life I was lucky to be born into. I tried to be brief, perhaps not too successfully. Talking about good times is often boring to people. Tolstoy phrased this notion more to the point: "All happy families are happy alike; every unhappy family is unhappy in its own way." Still I felt that I had to give some evidence of the good beginning, to outline the contrast to what happened later on.

I also experienced some scientifically inexplicable, disturbing, and recurring phenomena that haunted me on and off. Luckily for me, happy events washed them away.

I.

I still feel the touch of my father's hand as I clung to it as we walked on our Sunday mornings over the hills of Buda. It was not just the right warmth and dryness of that touch, it was much more; a safety, an assurance, a belonging, a nudge that everything was fine and always would be. Well, it was not. But at the time it gave me an indestructable feeling; it built a fortress in me that withstood everything and anything and that made me not just endure but overcome any difficulty in my life. It somehow made me inspect, consider, and contemplate the problems from a distance of time and place. But I'm running ahead of myself.

So, I return to that long-ago Sunday morning when the two of us were walking, after we got off streetcar #59 at the outskirts of Buda. We sometimes cut across the cemetery and Papa would stop here and there to read a touching inscription in memory of total strangers. One day he stopped with me in front of an unusual tombstone. It was a tall candle that, as he explained to me, indicated that the little girl, who died at age five as the inscription revealed, did not live her life, that it was cut short. I was not familiar with the term "symbolism"—I was only five or six at the time—but I understood the picture's meaning instantly. It must have made a strong impression on me or I would not remember it. I was very much touched by this art of expression. What it really meant to die so soon and not to live out one's life, I am sure I did not understand at the time.

I also got another impression from these peaceful walks through the cemetery, where the abundance of beautiful flowers created a picturesque sight among the shady trees whose foliages were gently swaying in the light breeze. It was never a frightful or scary place. I simply accepted that what was born had to die. The fact that my own great-grandmother's tombstone indicated that she lived from 1823 to 1921 and that my grandparents lived to a high age and in good health did not prepare me to find out that this was exceptional and that old age was or is not always as rosy as I have witnessed it within my own family. It seemed like eternity to live that long, and thus Death seemed so far away that I never thought of it in first person.

Well, it played a trick on me, and not just once. But here I go again. I had better retrace my steps before they run ahead of me.

Well, the inevitable happened. I grew up. I didn't want to. I fought it. I think I might have been afraid that I'd lose Papa's love, or was I intimidated by the opposite sex? Why? I saw plenty of men I loved in a sense. Like the old family doctor we had, for example, or a cousin I seldom saw, and many more. As a matter of fact I did yearn to meet the Right person, but it seemed that no one came close and I felt discouraged. To be truthful, several seemingly Right persons showed up, but I mistrusted them for no known reason. Afraid? But why? I worked out several theories; some might have been approaching me because of the family was a very good one and well situated, prestigious. That would indicate that I had no selfconfidence. I had, up to a point. What I wanted was different from what other girls aspired to. I imagined that a spiritual relationship would be ideal, which would dissolve eventually into the physical realm. Perhaps I would have found it among artists, should I have moved in such circles. Perhaps not. But when I met a few, mostly performing artists, not creative ones, I withdrew into my shell. No; more sobriety would be needed. I was far out enough. Did I subconsciously think that in order to have healthy children I needed a good balance? I don't really know why. One has more undercurrents than one is aware of. I give it a strong possibility.

Well, after all that self-doubt I went to a New Year's Eve celebration with an acquaintance of mine. The night was crisp and starlit; a light snow covered the streets and roofs of Budapest. The Danube we had to cross by bus looked dark and deep from the windows while the shores shone brilliantly on both sides. The dark masses of the *Gellért* and *Vár Hill* (Castle Hill) had fewer lights than the Pest side that sparkled like the many champagne glasses would that night, ushering in the New Year.

The party was not a big affair; I knew everybody. The place was little overcrowded, not just by the furniture that was on the dark side, rugs and drapes included, but by the guests. The huge Venetian glass mirror my girlfriend told me was her father's pride reflected the whirling guests, creating a somewhat unreal, distant look. Somebody played the piano. Jazz. I never liked it, but I danced to it just the same. Everything looked fine on the surface, but I was bored with it all. Then somewhat belatedly a new guest arrived whom I had never seen before. He was introduced to all as an old friend of the family who lived mostly abroad. I didn't catch just where. After a while they switched to records and the dancing went on. We also helped ourselves to the little sandwiches and refreshments offered by the family and we watched each other casually and critically. Then when a waltz was played, the stranger came over to me and asked me for this dance. He said it was his favorite if I would be willing. Actually the music was Dvorak's, a rare waltz I never heard before. No one else danced; they found it too old-fashioned. I was intrigued. I wasn't a particularly good dancer, I merely enjoyed the rhythms. But this gentleman gave me wings. I experienced a lightness I had never felt before. Was it Dvorak? Was it this stranger, or both? Or was it something else? I couldn't tell. I knew that I was not under the influence of drink as I barely touch it, just for appearance's sake. But I felt almost drunk after this dance. Everything was whirling around me even after I stopped. I had to hold on to the edge of a chair.

"Was I too fast?" he asked, concern in his voice. I just shook my head.

"It is a lovely piece," I heard myself declare, barely recognizing my own voice.

"Will you dance another waltz with me if they play one?" he asked.

"Yes," I said simply.

He looked very content. While he was munching on something he asked: "Would it be possible for us to meet again? I have only a few days in Budapest, though I plan on returning soon."

"Well," I said somewhat pensively: "It's New Year's Day tomorrow and we go to a poetry reading. Would you like to come along?"

"I'd like that very much but I would prefer to be just with you alone. Is that too much to ask? Besides tomorrow morning I have something to attend to."

"How about a walk then sometime?" I asked.

He turned around, looked at me puzzled: "A walk?"

"Yes, a walk." I laughed. "What's so unusual about it? Don't you walk? We always walk and talk, it is rather pleasant. One can get pretty well acquainted this way."

"How original!" he exclaimed. "I have expected you to say to go somewhere like a night club, or dancing at a fancy place. There are quite a few to choose from in this city."

"I know," I admitted, somewhat disappointed. "But I don't care for nightclubs at all. They are dull, often with vulgar singing, too much smoke. I prefer fresh air."

"All right, you convinced me, but how do you know that the nightclubs are dull if you don't visit them?"

Was he suspicious or did he wish to probe? I turned toward him: "If you wish to know, one of my best girlfriend's father owns one and we rather frequently go there if for a short time; it's like home practically. We know everybody, but I still don't care for the atmosphere."

He acknowledged that with a noncommittal "I see." He was to pick me up in front of my home two days later, early in the afternoon.

A few light and fluffy snowflakes floated in the air aimlessly, creating a pale bluish mist that hung over everything like a veil. It softened the contours of houses, people, streetcars, and lampposts into an Utrillo painting.

I was surprised how debonair he looked as he approached me. He was dressed in a sporty manner, but everything on him bespoke a careless-looking but selectively chosen elegance: his dark green Borzalino hat with a perky little colorful feather tucked into the ribbon, the woolen scarf matching the colors of the hat and feather in its subdued pattern. I especially loved his gray gloves. They were of the same soft deerskin, all handstitched, as Father's. I knew its touch intimately. His eyes shone with a warm smile and I could not quite decide under his somewhat bushy eyebrows if they were gray or greenish gray. He seemed to take in my attire equally well. I just got it for Christmas. It was a winter suit, golden brown with a leopard-skin collar and cuffs. I had a matching pert little rimless hat with it that gave the outfit a rather nicely finished touch. Mother chose it for me. She said it used to be her favorite color and it would suit me very well as I also had auburn hair and green eyes.

Oskar had the good taste not to say anything, but I saw in his eyes the appreciation of my fine-cut elegance.

"Which way?" he asked.

"Straight up," and I pointed toward a steep street.

The wild chestnut trees flanking this street created a veritable alley as the stately "arches" touched and seemed to be interwound in an intricate zig-zag, now lightly covered with fluffy snow. It looked more like the creation of an artist than nature's work. I thought it almost looked menacing; if it had been depicted on the cover of a book or used as stage decoration, I would have felt foreboding for what was to come.

We walked side by side along the fenced-in yards of the neighboring villas and talked and talked. When he found out that I liked opera, he suggested going there the night before he had to leave. I gladly agreed.

I did not see him the next few days as both of us were busy. As I was thinking of just how much I knew about him after our walk, I realized that it was very little. He made me talk a lot and found out quite a bit about me. I, on the other hand, had only an inkling of what he liked to read, what music he liked, and about his travels. Not much. I only realized this after mother had asked me who that good-looking young man was. She had seen us from the window as we walked up the street.

"Invite him for tea the next time you meet," she said.

I was astonished. Never had she taken any interest in any of the boys that came and went. Was it because this one was really a man, and not a mere "boy?" Or did she sense something I did not? I didn't know much about mothers' instincts, but I had my own stubborn opinions, often stemming from gut feelings or, if you please, sheer inexplicable intuition. And my feelings this time were totally unclear to me. He was gone and would not tell me exactly when he would be back. He said he would call as soon as he could. That was all. There I found too much secretiveness in this. A mistrust? No, I was sure of that. Perhaps it had to do with his line of work. That was it, I decided. For heaven's sake! Would he be a spy? Absurd. That's not the way spies act. Why not? I asked myself. How would I know? I had never met one, barely even read a book about them. But there was a war going on, after all, and although I did not feel its consequences yet in first person, one heard all kind of unpleasantness. Father took part in the First World War; he was too old for the Second one and I had no brothers. So far we had only experienced that certain items disappeared from the stores, but you could get almost anything on the black market.

I wasn't even sure if I would ever see Oskar again, but I had a rather pleasant memory of the evening at the Opera, except for one split-second of disturbance. As I approached the arcades by the main entrance, my eyes were searching for Oskar in the crowd. Cars and taxis were pulling up and swiftly gave way to the next. The light of one of them must have been crooked, as it threw a ray of light upward in an eerie way, and there it passed swiftly over Oskar's face in a bluish sheen, making him appear almost like a ghost. I called his name out loud, but in the tumult he did not hear me; presently he took notice of my waving hand and we joined each other.

We took our seats and enjoyed the usual hum of people talking, coming and going, the orchestra pit's din; an oboe here, a flute trilling there, a bassoon booming. Soon all the musicians entered and Sergio Faglioni's familiar frail figure approached the dais. He was the resident conductor, originally coming from Italy. He raised his baton and the ominous chords of *Rigoletto* filled the house.

We walked out during the intermission and I saw what a finely cut dark suit Oskar wore with a white silk-looking shirt and a deep red tie. I wore a black and dark-blue taffeta skirt with a white georgette blouse and a wide green velvet belt. Oskar's hair was parted on the side and was kind of medium brown. I made a point of looking at it as I was not quite sure. His strong masculine nose with delicate nostrils would have looked great on a baritone singer. His mouth was somewhat narrow, decisive, almost too strict-looking.

It was a memorable evening before Oskar's departure.

Days went by, busy days for the whole family and friends. I kept thinking of Oskar, wondering if he'd ever show up again. I was sure he would. I was looking forward to see him again. I was almost impatient. Was I perhaps in love? I didn't think so. Perhaps on my way there, I chided myself.

I knew that I had what you might refer to as a high boiling point. What I mean is this: I think of a classmate of mine, of whom we all knew that she had a real love affair with a young man; secretly, of course. The pictures she had shown a few of us were—although she was dressed—in such provoking poses that we just gaped at them when she proudly took them out to boast. Then a remark here or there. She would refer to a kiss as nothing, while most of us had not even been kissed yet. I am talking of fifteen, sixteen-year-old girls. Later on in life I referred to this young lady as a crocus, as she blossomed so early. While I myself, was definitely a chrysanthemum, a late, fall-blooming flower. There were a few more in the class who had "lived." How much, I don't know, but they were far from innocent, even if perhaps they didn't go all the way, out of fear. There was one particular girl whose "boiling point" was definitely very low. Any pants approaching would turn her on and she would roll her eyes and perhaps not just her eyes, until she was noticed. I am sure she rewarded those youngsters and they rewarded her in turn. She was what is usually known as a typical sexpot. I envied her a little but mostly I looked down on her, both at the same time. Don't ask me how that was possible because I don't know.

The first Friday of the month was approaching and that meant that Mother's chamber music group was to perform in our home. She played the violin or viola, according to need. I rarely participated, but I did when the piano was needed, like this time. Schubert's *Trout Quintet* was to be performed for our close friends who appreciated this kind of music-making. I also played the clarinet but seldom performed, until we found a friend's friend who was delighted to rewrite well-known pieces for the clarinet, to be incorporated in trios, or quartets. This was absolutely unique and delightful.

Our Bechstein piano was opened; the lovely off-white silk and lace coverlet from it that used to belong to my great-grandmother was carefully put away. The beautiful blue majolica vase that Father brought from somewhere abroad for Mother and that was always filled with fresh flowers was put on the floor, close to the large French doors opening to the rose-garden. At that time it was covered with a light snow blanket.

This music room was the pride of the whole family. Once Maman and Papa were invited into an Italian villa where they encountered a unique room in powder blue and white with a hint of gold and they both fell in love with the atmosphere it created. When Papa had the villa built, they decided to if not copy it, emulate it to suit their own taste. They had to have the proper wallpaper and the rug brought from abroad. The result was something exquisite. The thick blue carpet complimented the wallpaper that started above the white-lacquered wainscot. Tiny, finely etched patterns of a little white and even less gold repeated the woodwork and its golden edging. The furniture was also white-lacquered woods with powder-blue velvet upholstery. A few potted plants, mostly palms and ferns, were the only other decoration apart from a white marble bust of a Greek maiden's head. Galatea? No pictures. Maman's portrait, painted by Lipot Hermann, hung in the dining room where the wall had a light hazelnut shade, a nice contrast to the dark mahogany furniture. There, as in the rest of the house the floors were of oak, and covered by a variety of Persian carpets. Returning to the music room, it created its own ambiance. It commanded a hushed tone.

Well, as we were just about to start, Mitzi, one of the maids, rushed to me. I had a telephone call. My heart jumped into my throat. I knew it must be Oskar. I was right. He had just returned and was impatient to see me as soon as possible. I explained what was going on and he asked permission to drop by. I was delighted.

We started playing at our usual time. I gave instructions to Mitzi to let in such and such a person very quietly, even in the middle of the performance. And lo and behold, he arrived shortly before the singing trout song, which I played on the piano. I was a little nervous but soon the beauty of the music enveloped me and I became the trout wriggling in the bubbling brook trying to avoid the angler, who unfortunately for the trout, caught me at the end.

Oskar applauded vigorously with the others when we finished. I left the piano and Mother came up, so I introduced them; then Maman introduced him to the rest of the guests. There were refreshments. Mother sat down next to Oskar and engaged him in talking music. It turned out that he too played the piano and yielding to Mother's coaxing, he sat down. All eyes were on the good-looking young man who sat there as if he belonged there. He looked at us for a second. A hush fell over everybody and he started to play another Schubert piece: *Moments Musicaux*. It was lovely. He was the cynosure of all eyes. I actually felt as proud of him as if he had been my prize possession. Ridiculous, I hardly knew him.

Maman's friends would not stop and applauded and applauded. He looked somewhat puzzled. Then someone said quite loud, "Please, play some more."

So, that's what they wanted; with that thought spreading into a smile, he sat down again and turning to us, asked in a clear voice: "Would it bore you if I played another Schubert piece?"

A vehement applause was the answer and another voice was heard: "We have a regular Schubertiad evening, don't we?" Everybody laughed, then again all eyes focused on Oskar, as he put his hands on the keyboard.

He looked up once more and said: *"Fantasia in F-minor."*

He started. The very first notes already transposed all of us into another world, that of Schubert's, never in my life had I heard it or anything else played like this. It touched one's heart to the marrow, it spoke to you in an intimate, one-to-one basis. Oskar played with his eyes almost glued to the keyboard. Maybe his absorption was so complete that the physical surroundings stopped existing for him. Just once, in the middle of that piece, when that same melody was repeated later on, he looked up, straight into my eyes, expressing in them Schubert's complaints. An ominous foreboding shook me; an early death. No, I must have been thinking of Schubert, whose soul must have known the inevitable and was reflected in this fantasia, written in the last year of his life. It could not refer to Oskar. But it took me a while to overcome the shivering. Eventually his playing lulled me back to the beautiful music. I had regained my composure by the time he finished the piece. He got an ovation, if one may use this term about a handful of people. He deserved it.

That evening somehow sealed our relationship. It changed it into a bond, that although just created, felt as if it had been there for a long, long time. I had no doubts about it, that it was the magic of the music-making. It brought souls of the same feather together.

We drank the usual per-to. That meant that from then on we addressed each other in the familiar way, not the formal one. I felt extremely happy and almost as if I belonged to him. We saw each other every day. I did not hold back, pretending that I had something more important to do. Actually I cancelled everything possible to be free when he was, so some days we even met more than once. Kate, one of my closest girlfriends, scolded me that I didn't know how to behave, but I wouldn't listen to her.

Next time I had a chance I asked Oskar if he hadn't ever thought of making a career as a concert pianist. He smiled, a little sadly, I thought.

"Yes, my mother wanted it too, and I was preparing for it. I even gave a few private concerts, but then the winds of war were approaching and I felt obliged to enter the diplomatic service. Now you know. One day though, I hope, when all this is over, I'll give it another serious consideration. I promise."

"But why? Wouldn't you bring more happiness to people by playing to them?"

"Perhaps, but before people can be happy they have to be free, live in a free world. I am afraid that the black clouds that have gathered promise nothing good, but tremendous storms. For the time being you still have a good life here, the war has not touched you yet. When I travel around and gather information, it is hard to believe that anyone around would not be engulfed by it."

He sighed barely audibly, and went on: "I feel a moral obligation to fight in this war. I am not a soldier, I dislike sabers and uniforms. I do believe in decency and the need to fight for it. This mounting evil has to be defeated or the world will see worse than the Middle Ages. Luckily I belong to a neutral country, so I could choose to fight my own way, through negotiations and diplomacy." He turned to face me and smiled. "I hate to say all this, but perhaps you can understand now why I have to wait with those higher calls in life."

I understood. What am I saying? I did not understand. I only accepted his message. It didn't make me feel good, but there was nothing in me that could enable me to understand what he was talking about, so I let it go at that.

"You are pretty busy these days, young lady," said my father, looking at me during dinner. "Anything exciting taken your fancy that I should know about?"

Before I could open my mouth, mother intervened: "She is spending a great deal of time with that young man who played Schubert so well. Remember, you even remarked how you liked it, though you were busy in your room."

"Oh, so that's it. Do you like him, Kitten?" and he looked at me as if wanting to read my face, not just hear my answer.

"I find his company fascinating, that's all."

"I see. By the way what is he doing for a living?"

I was afraid he would ask that. I didn't want to look like a fool, but I had to admit that I wasn't really quite sure. "He is traveling a lot, mostly abroad," I added. "He also said that he was serving in the diplomatic service."

With that the subject was dropped. Papa reached for the bell that was hanging from the bronze chandelier right above the dining table. I loved this little acorn-shaped silver bell with its ivory button. Papa had brought this lovely objet d'art from somewhere, long before I appeared on the scene, so he told me.

The maid appeared and cleared the dishes away, making room for the dessert. We always ate very well. It was very important to Father, and Maman saw to it that his every wish was fulfilled.

Papa was a very successful businessman, owning his company. He adored Maman and treated her like a fragile gift. They used to take trips not just to nearby Austria, where we often spent our summer holidays together, but for ten days or two weeks to Italy or Switzerland. They would always bring home exquisite gifts. Whenever they were gone I was left in the care of Auntie Caroline, who lived with her husband in the basement apartment of our villa. Her husband worked for Papa and lived rent-free in our home. They had no children. They were in charge with a variety of things to do for us and in turn they had a choice home and yard the like of which they could have never afforded. Papa was richly rewarded with a trusted employee. They also had a built-in baby sitter in Aunt Caroline, who cared for me as her own child; she lavished all her maternal feelings on me. I loved her dearly.

When I was still a little girl, Maman told me that she was going to take me to the *Tabán*, a section of town in Buda, so I might see it before they demolished it. Our washerwoman lived there. So did another stout woman who came to help out only occasionally. Maman had some gifts wrapped and we were going to leave those with them. I saw there small houses and huts huddled together in extremely narrow, cobblestone streets. Children clad in rags were playing in the gutter. A smell of cabbage and boiled potatoes mixed with an unsanitary odor lingered all over the place. The faces I encountered on the adults were pale and grim, as if sunshine had never penetrated those streets. The house where the washerwoman lived was surprisingly interesting, full of stone statues. They were in the small yard, around the windows, at the entrances, on the facade of the house. Maman explained to me that a sculptor had lived there in the previous century and left behind the fruits of his imagination and labor.

"They are not unhappy faces," I remarked, referring to the statues, "like those on the street, but rather funny ones. Perhaps they tell us some funny secrets."

I don't really remember having said this, but Maman repeated it so often to friends that I was made aware of it how amusing it must have sounded to the adults. Then Mother went on, explaining that not everybody lived as well and happily as we and most of our friends did, but that there was a lot of poverty and misery in this world.

"So, as they say: *noblesse oblige*. Remember it, my little darling; if you are lucky and well situated it is your duty to help the less fortunate. You often see me and our friends fixing up packages, all sort of food, clothing, also toys, especially before Christmas. We all work together to send it and give it to those who need it very badly. You will do it too, when you grow up, won't you?"

I nodded my head in agreement. I felt very sorry particularly for those children.

As soon as we got home I went to my room and climbed up on a chair to reach the top of the built-in closet, where a lot of my toys were that I seldom played with. I took them all down, went to one of the maids, and asked for a large box. I returned with it and filled it to the brim. Then I looked for Maman and called her to my room. Pointing at the box, I asked her:

"Will that do? Would those children take it?"

Mother took one look at me, one at the box. She wiped a tear from her eye and kissed me on my forehead. "It will. I can see you understood what *noblesse oblige* means."

I recall vividly another incident rather early in my life. We walked by a fancy candy store somewhere in town and Papa asked me if I wanted some bonbons. Now he knew that I loved them as well as everything sweet. Still somehow I declined the offer with a firm "thank you, no." I happened to look up at his face and saw a most contented smile spread all over it. This to me seemed much much sweeter than if all the world's chocolates had melted in my mouth. I instinctively felt that self-denial or discipline would please him and I would have done anything to gain his approval.

II.

Oskar was out of town again. I missed him terribly. I began to feel an attachment I had never known before, especially not to someone I had just rather recently met. I still couldn't say it was love; then, he never told me he loved me, but there was a mutual something between us that was deeper—so I felt, at least—than words can tell or that was "justified" by the brief encounters. I knew him well enough, or perhaps I should say, I sensed, that he was not one to commit himself fast or easily, if at all. Then there was that business of his that he had barely hinted at, his being in the diplomatic service. Whose diplomatic service? What side? I shouldn't have posed the latter question to myself. Surely he could not be on the Axis' side. That was out of the question. I was convinced of that. If I wanted to reassure myself that my so called political judgment was right—and I needed this reassurance, as I was as apolitical as you can be—I only had to think of the fact that Oskar was a close friend of Vera's family and their political standing was clear. Her father was a close friend of my father. That alone told me that Oskar must have similar convictions.

While I occupied myself with the rehearsals for Verdi's *Requiem*—I sang in the choir—I had to make sure that my brown robe was getting ready. On my way to the dressmaker's house I ran into Vera. By the way, the robe looked like the ones the monks wore who lived in a cloister carved into the rocks on the Danube side of Mt. Gellert, not very far from our home. The brown robe suited Verdi more than the usual black habits, so we all decided in their favor.

"How is Oskar?" asked Vera, grinning at me knowingly.

"How should I know?" I retorted. "He left and I don't even know where to. As far as I am concerned, he might never even show up again."

I said all that deliberately, as I was annoyed at the evident gossip going the rounds.

"Don't give me that," and she looked at me straight in the eye with those large blue pools she turned men's heads with. "If anyone, you ought to know something," and she laughed self-assuredly and impishly at the same time.

As I did not respond and she felt my resistance, her curiosity must have been piqued. She took my arm and started to walk with me to the dressmaker.

I didn't mean to be rude, but I knew that whatever I told her I might as well have stood in the largest square in Budapest and shouted it to the people. So after we left, she told me that she was about to call me anyway.

I glanced at her and noticed how chic she looked. I always envied her good figure and how she could make herself appear in the best possible light. Clothes had a lot to do with it, but I also had good clothes. There was more to it, a certain taste, not to subdue one's appearance, but to enhance it; well, sex appeal. It is hard to put it into words or analyze it. You simply had to look at her, and there it was. You sensed it. Small wonder she was so popular and looked, how should I put it, more like a ripe fruit that was more appealing than a bud with only a promise. The bud of course is in reference to an innocent young lady. I, with a few others of our girlfriends, suspected that she was really living with someone. We had no proof.

"I just talked to Kato," Vera went on, "and she agreed to come to a Gypsy woman to have our fortunes told. Come along with us; it'll be fun."

"You are not serious," I answered. "You don't really believe in such nonsense?"

"Who said I believe it?" she grinned. "I merely said it was going to be fun. Kato also thinks it is going to be interesting."

"Who else is going?" I asked.

"I think Kato's mother showed interest."

"I can hardly believe this. Anyway, where in the world did you find her and where does she live?" I asked.

"She is not one of those Gypsies who live in the Gypsy camps outside of the city. I wouldn't go there, but she has a regular apartment in one of those new modern buildings in the outskirts that they just recently built. I also heard that she does not look or dress like a Gypsy at all. Perhaps she just says that she is one to earn more credibility for her hocus-pocus. But they all agreed that she was fabulous."

"All right, why not, it won't hurt me" I agreed.

I didn't want to seem like the stuffed shirt they often called me behind my back.

"When do we go? I asked.

"We made an appointment with her for this Thursday. Why don't you come, pick me up, and we go together. We'll meet Kato with her mother there."

We parted and I rushed home. There were two postcards for me. Greetings from Oskar. One could hardly make out the signature. One came from Switzerland, and the other from Sweden, with one week's difference in the dates. *He sure gets around,* I thought. Then it hit me. Both of those were neutral countries. He must be in contact with them somehow. There was no return address on either of them.

"I see you got mail from abroad?" greeted my mother.

So, she saw them.

"Who from?" she asked.

"You mean, you didn't read the cards?" and I looked at her quite astonished.

"Of course, I glanced at them but I could not decipher those hieroglyphs. Would those be Oskar's signatures? Did he say where he was going?"

"No, but since I don't know anyone in either country, with a little stretch of the imagination one could fancy it to be Oskar. Who else?" I laughed and thought that the brief greetings with the illegible signature was in keeping with his secretiveness.

Thursday arrived and we burst upon the soothsayer's place almost simultaneously with Kato and her mother. The three of us girls went in rather high spirits. Kato's mother was a little nervous. I couldn't imagine her taking anything like that seriously.

The so-called Gypsy woman was a tall, flat-chested nondescript apparition in a very simple frock. After greeting us at the door, she ushered us into a room where the focal point was a square table with a deck of cards on it. A sofa boasted some colorful pillows stitched in a variety of Hungarian folk art. The sole indication that this was not an ordinary abode came from the presence of a large stuffed owl eyeing us with one eye, the other being shut. Two candles on the sideboard gave one the feeling that perhaps they had seances there too. I had no proof of that. It was merely a fleeting impression.

She motioned for us to sit down around the table. She took the largest chair; evidently that was hers; it was facing the owl and I forgot to mention a skull too that looked grim, not at all grinning, as some of them do.

"I am going to read your palms first, then the cards, if that is agreeable to you. This is my usual custom."

We nodded in agreement and a little suspense stole into the room on silent and invisible feet.

Vera was sitting across from her. She, perhaps quite involuntarily stretched her hand out, and the woman took it. She looked a while, frowned, and let the hand go.

"Why did you remove your wedding ring? To deceive me?"

Vera stiffened and tried to laugh it off. "But I don't have a wedding ring, I am not married."

"Strange," murmured the woman. "Your palm shows definite indication of your being married."

Then she went on. We could hardly pay attention to whatever else she had said, so hard was it for us to contain our calm. So, the woman saw in Vera's palm what we had only suspected for quite some time now.

The next "victim" was Kato's mother. Looking at her hand, the woman turned pale and it took a while before she spoke: "Ma'am, you are going to lose your husband within a year."

The mother bit her lips. Perhaps she thought that the blond singer from the nightclub was going to take him away from her, or someone else? Her husband was known to be a philanderer on the sly. Finally she mustered enough courage to ask a simple question: "How?"

"Oh, didn't I tell you? By death. I am really sorry."

At that the lady laughed out loud in a shrieking sound that made us shiver. The news was sudden, cruel, but did not touch us as badly as her reaction to it. We simply did not believe it; neither did she.

When the woman read Kato's palm she only said that it would be several years before she was going to get married.

Next I turned my palm up and into her hand. I didn't like the touch. It was icy and almost feeling as if you had touched an amphibian. But I held it and waited.

"You ought to learn lots of languages, my dear. You'll need them."

There was some more talk of no consequence. We paid and left. Upon leaving this house I said in a casual voice, "I don't think it was worth our while to come, she fed us a lot of rubbish."

They all agreed and we parted. I didn't mention the incident at home. I would have been ashamed. Besides, I did not want to bring up Vera's situation. They might have asked a few questions, and I am not a very good liar. It was bad enough to know that her cousin just eloped the previous week with a man who had gotten her pregnant. Vera related all this to me, and also that after they went on their honeymoon they wired home that they got married. It's needless to say how upset the family was because of the scandal and because they were deprived of being able to have a big wedding with all the trimmings for their lovely daughter. What was interesting about it to us was that this young lady's brother was the one who was Vera's friend, the secret lover.

Vera, by the way, never brought up the incident with the so called Gypsy woman and we did not wish to embarrass her, so no one spoke of it. As far as Kato's mother was concerned, she did lose her husband, quite unexpectedly. He was forty-six years old and in perfect health.

III.

One day when I got home, a note by the telephone said that Oskar had called and I should return the call at such and such a number. My heart was pounding. I recognized Auntie Caroline's handwriting and wanted to know what else he had said before I called. I ran down the long hallway, down the stairs, and rushed to her door. The whirring of the sewing machine told me that she was in. I burst into the room. She just smiled as she looked up from her work and winked good-naturedly. "So, that's how we stand. What would you like to know, my little precious?"

"Did you talk to Oskar?" I asked, quite out of breath.

"Yes, of course."

"What else did he say?" I asked impatiently.

"Well, let me see. He asked for you and when I told him that you were not home he asked if he was talking to your mother. I said she wasn't home either and that I was the housekeeper. Then he left the message. That's all."

"Thanks a lot, Auntie." I hugged her, ran back to the phone, and dialed. He answered himself.

"Thank God you called, Agi, I began to wonder if you ever would. I was just about to leave full of worries that you have forgotten me."

"Not a chance," I answered.

"When can I see you?" and he added before I had time to answer, "as soon as possible, please."

"I just came home. Would you like to come over or do you have something else in mind?"

"Actually I'd love to come over, but I also would like to talk to you kind of privately. Now, don't laugh, could we perhaps walk a while, and then I come in?"

"Sure, that sounds fine. Is everything all right? You sound rather serious."

"Everything is all right," he reassured me, although he did not quite convince me. "Would it be too much trouble if you came to the hotel, we could meet in the lobby and simply walk over across the bridge and straight up the hill."

"I'll grab my coat and be there in twenty minutes," I promised.

I rushed to my room, powdered my nose, took my coat and took off.

After I crossed the bridge by bus and reached the Pest side, I got off and walked toward the Hotel Hungaria. I walked over that large round car-turntable that I had loved to watch as a child. Once a car arrived, it could not turn around because of the narrow space. So this "lazy susan" turned around, and voilà, the car was facing town and could take off. I turned the corner, went toward the main entrance, and entered the marble-covered elegant lobby.

Oskar spotted me instantly—he must have had his eyes on the revolving doors. He greeted me cheerfully: "You're even more beautiful than I remembered you." This was the first time he had paid me a compliment and I was a little embarrassed, but happy. He wrapped his shawl around his neck, donned his coat and hat, and off we walked into the street. The hotel porter, wearing the customary green uniform, bowed deeply.

It was late February and a rather mild, clear day. The seagulls circled around the bridge and swooped down to the water and back again. They would screech in B-flat major and the taxi horns seemed to answer them an octave deeper at random intervals.

There were no streetcars going across the Chainbridge, but plenty of buses and taxis and also passers-by. There was also a promise of spring in the air; an intangible element that one felt with one's nose and skin. Once we reached Buda we did not go through the tunnel, but turned left, walking along the Danube Quai toward Mt. Gellert. The Danube shone almost blue, which does not happen often. It reflected the clear sky, The water's metallic-looking surface reminded one that just recently broken ice pieces were floating on it. There was no trace of snow around anymore. Perhaps we were in for an early spring. That would be certainly nice, especially now that Oskar was back. I wondered how long he might stay this time.

We walked along the lower quai where we seemed to be by ourselves. He took my arm. I let him. It felt good. We both glanced across the Danube where the Parliament building sprawled majestically in its neo-Gothic splendor.

"It feels so good to be with you again, dearest Agi," he said, breaking the silence.

I had been dreaming of and waiting for this moment.

"I was so busy," he went on. "Did you get my cards?"

I turned toward him with a poker face: "So it was you who had written."

"You mean you had any doubt? Do you know other people in Zürich or Stockholm?"

"Sure, lots of them," I said impishly.

He laughed. "Agi," he said, his voice a little strained, "I thought of you a lot and I have to admit that I missed you terribly. I knew the minute I first met you that you're someone special, but I didn't know how special. I never met anyone like you and I have to admit that I fell in love with you. I hope I do not embarrass you by being so blunt."

I was all smiles. I would have liked to hug him, but I had to wait for him. I wished it had been dark. Perhaps he had the same thought, as he pointed toward the Fishermen's Bastei, a promenade dug into the side of the hill, zig-zagging upwards with stone benches here and there. It was too cold to sit down yet. We found a nice secluded place under the Romanesque stone arches flanking the esplanade on both sides. No one was in sight and he pulled me toward him and kissed me. First tenderly, then as I did not fight him, with more vehemence.

"I love you, Agi, more than I can tell you. Do you feel anything toward me?"

I don't know what came over me, I put aside all modesty and pretense, and blurted out: "I do love you, Oskar. I didn't know until now, I merely suspected it. I was also waiting for your return impatiently."

He kissed me again and again and hugged me and we walked again without words.

"You made me the happiest man on earth, Agi."

We stepped in unison, arm in arm and felt content with each other and the world.

The next few weeks went by too fast. We were on cloud nine. We went to the opera again, to concerts; we saw some movies. More often than not we ended up in our favorite place, a pastry shop close to the Elizabeth Bridge.

To go to pastry shops is a favorite pastime in Central European countries; just like going to coffee houses. Vienna established the coffeehouses in the late seventeenth century and the vogue spread over the whole Austro-Hungarian Empire. So there were pastry shops dotting the boulevards and side streets.

Oskar came to the house too. He participated in another chamber music soirée, to everybody's delight. Even Father talked to him briefly and was favorably impressed, although he had no idea how serious we were about each other. I believe Mother suspected it, but since I said nothing about any future plans, she kept silent. I think she had approved of him wholeheartedly. I could see it in her behavior toward him. Auntie Caroline told me openly that she thought that this young man was perfect for me. I hugged her. She had always approved of anything I ever did. She had really spoiled me.

The day arrived when Oskar told me that he had to leave once again. He added this time that he was never sure himself just how long his duties would keep him away. But he reassured me that he'd come as soon as possible. He also said that he could only write post cards, greetings. Then finally he admitted that he worked for the government in both Switzerland and Sweden and it had something to do with partly the Red Cross, and partly trying to save and rescue people from the clutches of the Nazis. He asked me not to mention anything of the sort to anyone. He was in the Diplomatic Service, and that should be sufficient for anyone to know. I promised and kept my word. He must have trusted me infinitely or he wouldn't have volunteered that much.

I felt an immense pride that he stood up and tried to do something against the ever-growing evils that engulfed most of Europe. I began to feel guilty for the life I had while millions suffered, although I didn't even suspect at the time how and how much.

Kato called me. She wanted to meet Oskar. She invited us to the nightclub I mentioned before. When I told her that he was gone, she wanted me to come anyway.

"You know, Agi, I am really getting bored with Andi all alone, we had so much more fun when we were a foursome."

"I thought you said you wanted to meet Oskar." I laughed.

"But of course. That's the main reason, the other is the secondary one."

"I don't really see why you waste your time with Andi if he offers nothing, if you're bored."

She interrupted me: "Neither were you really interested in Nicky, or any other boy you dated on and off."

"True, but I did not hold on too long either. Just to go out with someone occasionally. I feel it is a necessity. One cannot find one's true love instantly. Some people never find it."

"Did you find it, Agi?"

"I think so."

"I'm very glad for you. But, please come if for old times' sake. Bring anyone you want, or if you wish I'll call someone."

"All right, if it means that much I'll come with, say, Bandi. You always liked him. Perhaps we can switch him over to you."

"Matchmaker?" she laughed.

"Just kidding."

Well, we had our foursome and it was a rather blah evening. It might be that I missed Oskar and only his company was good enough for me now.

After quite a long interval, Oskar called again. This time he took a room in the Hotel Gellert to be closer to me, and we spent as much time together as possible. He came often to the house now.

Our villa did not face the street. When you entered the fence gate, you were standing at the back of the house. There was a large entry, but the real facade of the house was on the yard side, away from the street. Not much was seen of anything from the street as a privet hedge grew tall on the inside of the fence and even before it reached its height, two stately linden trees, one on each side, blocked the view. The dark green shiny leaves of this hedge were so fragrant that any time whenever a whiff of a privet hedge reached my nostrils, later on in my life, it had the power to transport me back in time and space to our home, ah so long ago, almost in another lifetime.

Papa insisted on having a modest front, but the back side was something very special. A huge white stone terrace with rounded steps toward the yard was adjacent to the music room and a rose garden consisting of two beds facing each other lengthwise, about ninety degrees to the house. Flagstones made walking easy between them. I often encountered little green lizards chasing each other there when I was little. They somehow disappeared later on, or I grew less observant. A few white stone benches were inviting-looking, placed by the lilac and hazelnut bushes framing the large lawn. The rose garden boasted of pink and crimson roses alternating with white and pale yellow ones. In between were tall sky-blue and deep-blue delphiniums. They seemed to dance in the light summer breeze to a melody all of their own. As Maman had designed the whole show, her friends often teased her that she actually "orchestrated" it. They even asked her what key she "wrote" them in. And she answered them without batting an eyelash, in total earnestness: "F-major, naturally. Can't you hear it? Sometimes it turns into A-major," she went on, "when the sun is high and the colors are their brightest, full of life, vibration and happiness."

Who knows what the friends thought of that, but they all loved the beauty of it, just as we did.

It was late May when Oskar came back. The air was fragrant with the perfumes of flowers. Oskar was enchanted with our yard.

"What a paradise this is, Agi. I wish my mother could see it, she would love it."

This was the first time he spoke of his family.

"Mother also has flowers in her yard, but the season in Sweden is shorter than here, although she has a summer home in Lund, in the south where it is milder than in Stockholm."

He stopped a second, as if he had been back home up North, with a faraway look on his face. Then he continued: "Did I tell you that she comes from Hungary? Only my father was Swedish; he died several years ago, before I grew up."

"I am so sorry," I said. "Do you remember him well?"

"Of course. He impressed upon me the importance of being in the diplomatic service. It was his idea and I feel the responsibility and weight of it in these troubled times very strongly. But I did promise Mother to return to the piano after this war is over. And I will."

By this time we were on the verandah that was facing the flower garden. We were having coffee and cakes. Mitzi served us from Mother's choice service, the midnight blue Rosenthal porcelain set with the golden lacy trims and little golden mocha spoons. I made the little marzipan loaves myself. He loved it and couldn't get over that I knew how to make them.

"It's Mother's recipe, rather easy," I admitted.

"What an incredibly lucky break it was for me that you happened to be at Vera's party when I visited them, or else we might have never met. By the way, are you a close friend of hers?"

"Not very very close, but we do get together and move in the same circles."

"She is a nice person," Oskar said. "Certainly good-looking, just a little too flirtatious in my book. The family is a good one, though, and perhaps she will slow down once married." He turned toward me: "Could I see your room, Agi?"

"Of course, come," and I led him up the stairs to my room, which also looked towards the yard, but on the side of the house. With the open windows the fragrance of spring penetrated and permeated it.

"It looks like you, Agi, a little serious, still friendly and inviting."

Actually it was not a very large room. I had a *recamier*—a divan—like bed couch—with pillows; the bedding was hidden in the built-in box at its bottom. Above it on the wall ran bookshelves filled to the brim; next to it a lamp for night reading. On the opposite wall was a combination of closets for clothes, shelves, and drawers, and also a so-called secretary that when opened, created a table on which I could write my schoolwork; when closed, it was flush with the rest. A bay window with cushioned seats looked upon the yard. Two chairs and a large rug completed the furnishings. That was all. It was sufficient for all my needs.

"I love it, just as I love you, Agi."

He came to me and kissed me and kissed me and would not let me go.

"I think that when we are married, you should have a blue and white room, like the one downstairs; it suits you and to me it represents heaven by its color and its atmosphere."

I was floored. Was that a proposal? Or it just slipped out? He saw the consternation on my face, and sat down in the window seat, pulling me towards him, real close.

"I do wish to marry you, Agi, I could not live without you anymore. You epitomize much more for me than I ever dreamt of finding. Please, say yes, I need you and I hope I can fulfill your dreams."

He kissed me again, as if afraid that I would suddenly evaporate from his clutches and from his life. I was so taken aback, so surprised, I was speechless for just a moment. We hardly knew each other, really. But I knew him enough to know that he was the most wonderful man I had ever met and ever hoped to meet. So I said, "Oskar, I did not consider myself ready for marriage yet, but since you came into my life,

I guess you changed all that. I would be very happy to spend the rest of my life at your side."

We hugged and hugged. He murmured a "thank you."

After a while of enjoying each others' kisses and embrace, he asked me if I wished to let my parents know or should he do it.

"I know, of course, that it is my part to play. However, I think it prudent if we waited till the end of the war. With my comings and goings it would be the right thing to do. You would wait for me, Agi, wouldn't you?"

"Yes, Oskar, I think this is a very good plan. I'll talk to Maman and then you may talk to them."

Maman was delighted. She loved that man. How could she not, after having heard his playing. His soul was in it and that revealed the man. Papa was more cautious.

"What do we know about him? Can he support you in the style you were brought up in, or at all, for that matter? I'm not saying I don't like him or don't trust him. As a matter of fact, he made a very favorable impression on me and I don't overlook the fact that Maman likes him so much, but after all you're our only child and I want to be sure that you'd be well taken care of. This isn't too much to ask, is it?"

Well, his doubts or rather lack of knowledge of Oskar and his background were taken care of by none other than Oskar himself. He was invited for dinner next Saturday. We always ate at one-thirty sharp. Oskar came sooner, as asked, so Papa might talk to him. Papa wasn't home yet, so I showed him the library. He stopped in front of a picture—I had a hunch he would. It was a self-portrait by Arnold Böcklin. It represented the artist holding his pallette as if painting in the company of Death, depicted by a violin-playing skeleton. It gave the impression that Death was suggesting some theme to him. I was so used to it that I never gave it a second thought, other than wondering what music he might be playing. The answer came to me many many years later when I got acquainted with Mahler's music. I was convinced that the skeleton played Mahler's music and Böcklin listened attentively.

But, returning to this great day in my life—Papa finally came and the two of them withdrew into the library. Later on Papa related to us all that Oskar had told him.

"Sir, with all due respect, before I ask you for the hand of your daughter in marriage, I have to tell you a few things about myself, as I am a stranger here. My family has ample means and I inherit it all, as I am an only child. My father died several years ago. Mother manages our business and the estate. She is a very capable woman. In order for you to see that I am telling the truth I took the liberty of bringing along some official papers and documents. Here is a letter written by me to our banks. Herein I gave them instruction to furnish you with all the information you'd require about my financial situation."

Here he stopped a minute, shifted his legs, and went on:

"Furthermore, the fact that I am working is that I cannot simply live off the fat of the land, even if it belongs to me. I have to have a responsibility other than that. So I chose the diplomatic service upon my late father's insistence. I work directly with the Swiss and Swedish Red Cross on behalf of the war effort, hence all my traveling. And this brings up what I explained to Agi, that it might be wise to wait with our marriage until the end of the war. She accepted it and I do hope you both will agree to it. I don't think I have to emphasize how much I love your daughter, how highly I think of her and how lucky I consider myself that we met and that she returns my love."

Father also told us, what he answered to Oskar. Here it is:

"Young man, I am very much impressed by you. To play the piano as you did, you must have a feeling soul; to work when you don't have to, shows great responsibility, and finally that you yourself offered to wait with the marriage till the end of the war—may it come soon—shows me your great care and discipline. I am very happy to have you for an in-law."

They shook hands and emerged beaming, heading toward the dining room.

The table was covered with a white damask tablecloth and matching napkins. The porcelain dishes were ivory-colored with a gold rim at the edge. Lilac with white lilies were cut short to create the centerpiece. The first course consisted of a soup. Papa always wanted soup, even in summertime. This one had liver dumplings in it, fluffy and light. It was followed by duck à l'orange for the main course, served with tiny new potatoes tossed in parsley butter and a piquant-tasting blue cabbage salad with a sweet-sour taste and raisins. Small caraway buns were arranged in a basket, with a light sparkling wine and fresh water. Maman and myself did not care for any wine. We had a mocha-cream torte for dessert and black coffee taken in the parlor. The conversation was light and happy. Oskar pulled a small package from his pocket and came to me. All eyes were glued to this object. He undid it and pulled out a gorgeous ring with an emerald stone.

"To match your eyes, I chose this, Agi. I hope it won't take long before we can exchange wedding rings."

He kissed my hands and my forehead. I returned his kiss on the cheek.

"It is beautiful, thank you."

"I am going to write to my mother tonight of this happy occasion. I know she'd be delighted. I also know she will come here as soon as it is going to be feasible. And I would like to take Agi with me to show her where I grew up. Mama talks Hungarian, so there won't be any difficulty in communicating."

Maman turned to Oskar: "Does your mother also play an instrument?"

"Oh yes, we all played something. Her favorite is the flute."

"How delightful," smiled Maman.

IV.

Oskar was coming and going. Each time we were together we were unbelievably happy to be in each other's company. One day he surprised me.

"Agi, I believe it would be a good idea if I took you to both the Swiss and Swedish Embassies to introduce you to the consul as well as some of the employees. It could happen that I cannot write you or it wouldn't reach you, but I could always send you letters in the diplomatic pouch of one or another person there. And if you wanted to reach me for whatever reason, then again you could only do that through the embassy."

"All right," I agreed. "You are certainly a circumspect person, I have to say that for you."

"Just that I don't want either of us be in a situation that we could not reach each other. It would be awful." After a while he added, "Another thing, Agi. I would like you to have my mother's name and address and not just on a piece of paper, but memorize it. One never knows. A paper might get lost. Mother would always be informed of my whereabouts, so that would be an important thing. All right?"

"Sure, anything you say."

I thought that this man surely tried to take care of everything. He didn't overlook a thing.

Time was flying when we were together and stood still when he was away. At one of his stays he played Schubert pieces for me again, the *Valses Nobles*.

"Those were times I would have preferred to live in, in Vienna, and with you. I feel so close to that, as if it had been part of my life," he said.

I asked him to play it again; I could not get enough of it. I honestly think that Schubert himself could not have played them with more emotion and proper expression. His soul must have flown into Oskar through the music.

The war was raging on all fronts and one heard awful stories. One couldn't tell what was true and what was rumor. But one could see that Hitler was in for great defeat and Allied victory would come. Rommel was chased from Africa in November 1942. The German troops reached Stalingrad. Fights around the city started in August 1942 already. It was slow progress and one of the bitterest fights in the history of this war, as the truth slowly transpired. Once they penetrated the city they had to fight from house to house, such was the resistance. On February 2, 1943 Stalingrad fell; what remained of it was again in the hands of the Russians. The Germans under the leadership of General Paulus were trapped. Paulus surrendered instead of committing suicide, although Hitler promoted him to field marshal. No German field marshal had ever surrendered before.

Next summer, it was in July, Mussolini was through. Even the blind could see by then what the outcome of the war was to be. It was almost euphoric just thinking of it.

The political atmosphere had changed tangibly in Hungary. The climate of the war took a sudden, almost incredible change. Newspapers started publishing Allied communiques, albeit under Stockholm datelines. Forced labor camps in Hungary were dissolved. One sergeant told his unit, "Fellas, we're not going to the front—the front is coming to us."

And indeed one glance at the map in the newspapers brought home the continuous retreat of the hitherto invincible German Army. As though by magic, the late night news were broadcast in French and English once again.

Still it was too early for rejoicing. One day, for example, as I was seeing Oskar off on the Eastern Railroad Station, I saw a train arrive. Oskar had just left and I somehow lingered around to still feel his closeness, even if his train was already long out of sight. There was a tumult of civilians, soldiers, heaps of bundles on which people slept in corners. The ground was littered; cleaning went slowly, though they made an effort. I spotted a family, at least they looked like a father, mother, and two teenagers. They were talking animatedly of meeting their returning son from the front. Soon the train bringing injured soldiers from the Ukraine huffed into the station. When it came to a halt the family rushed up and down alongside its carriages, searching the windows for their son. Lots of shabby-looking, unshaven, bandaged soldiers filled the windows. The parents shouted their son's name loud. Then two soldiers descended right by them carrying a clothes-basket. In it sat a human being, or rather what was left of one. Half of both arms were missing, no legs. I glimpsed this unfortunate sight and turned away and ran. I barely managed not to get sick. It was something awful. And that was just one single incident. I could never forget it. It haunted me with those glaring, glassy eyes. Merciful God, his death would have been a blessing for that young man and his family too.

One day Maman read aloud from the newspaper's obituary column: This is to announce that my beloved husband burnt to death, trapped in a tent somewhere between the Don and Dnieper Rivers. They tried to concoct a gas for burning, to enable them to see in the dark, long winter nights. A few chemists were sure to help their comrades. They failed. Farewell my beloved, your wife and your little son you never laid eyes upon.

The English teacher, where I took classes twice a week, left. He was sent to a forced labor camp, picking mines in the Ukraine. Not two weeks had passed since his departure, when his glasses were returned to his wife. That was all that remained of him.

Frightening news circled about these forced labor camps, where sadistic brutalities took place. One hoped against hope that they were not true. As it turned out, what took place was much worse than any rumor that reached the homeland.

There was a Polish family who fled and somehow managed to get settled in Budapest. They had a three-year-old daughter who cried and screamed each Saturday at one P.M. when the sirens wailed. They were turned on every week since the beginning of the war, for practice. No one paid attention to it, one got used to it. But that little girl remembered the bombing, the running to the shelter, the nervousness of the grownups, and she was frightened out of her wits, even if no bombs fell and no running followed. She associated the sound with her fright and no one could calm her down and explain that this was just exercise. She was too young to understand this. But she was not too young to understand the horror of it.

My grandfather got sick and needed an operation; it turned out to be cancer. He was calm; he only told me once that he would like to see the end of Hitler. He did not. He died rather suddenly and my dear grandmother, though there was nothing wrong with her physically, followed him within two weeks. She could not live without him, so they said. They were both in their high eighties. Maman was very sad; they were her parents. To occupy herself she plunged into more and more charity work.

Father had a very old aunt living in the country and we were about to go to see her. I caught a very bad cold; besides I was waiting impatiently for Oskar, so my parents left by themselves, just for a few days.

As my cold got worse, Auntie Caroline took care of me. When the regular remedies failed to nurse me back to health, she said she had something very special that always did the trick, if I agreed to it.

"What is it?" I asked.

"The *dodanella;* it is a simple herb. I brew a tea from it. It is very beneficial for lots of things, mostly against cold of a more severe nature. Occasionally it would ease even pneumonia."

I thought that this was ridiculous, but what could an herb harm? At its worst, it would taste bad. I had no intention of hurting her feelings.

"By the way you can't get *dodanella* here. I have some left from the last package I got from my sister," she said.

"Ah, is this the one who lives in Transylvania?" I asked.

"Right, she picked it herself for me in the fall. She knows where to find it; it is rather scarce. I believe the only other place where it grows is in Slovakia, also in the Carpatian Mountains. But I don't know that it also has this rare quality of curing ills. Then again, who knows?"

She left the room and came back some time later with a cup full of the piping hot tea. I sat up to take it from her. It had a pungent odor, not unpleasant, but not exactly appetizing either. Still, it reminded me of a mixture of camomile tea and thyme. They also grew in those regions, I heard her say when I was a child and was forced to drink the tea when sick. It seemed it also had a touch of the tartness of the red whortleberry. But altogether it had an unpleasant bitterish aftertaste that was not characteristic of any of those by themselves. Well, I drank the whole cup and perhaps from the hot tea I got very sleepy. She turned my light off and withdrew; I fell into a deep oblivion.

Suddenly I heard some noise, and woke up, sitting up in my bed and kind of not knowing where I was. Then I saw Auntie Caroline with another steaming cupful of the same concoction.

"What, another?" I asked, a little annoyed, trying to wipe the sleep from my eyes. "What time is it?"

"You slept some two hours, and I thought I would bring another one before I retire for the night," she said, handing me the cup. I drank it dutifully and she left. I hardly had strength in my arm to reach for the light switch that she forgot to turn off this time. I also felt a strange sensation in both of my temples. Something pulled inside of them. Most unusual. *That must have been some potent tea,* I thought, and with that I went to sleep once again.

V.

"Darling, you're sure sleeping in late, do you feel well?"

"Oskar? When did you come back?"

"Back from where?"

"Well, I am not quite sure. What are you doing here?"

"What an odd question; I am shaving to get ready for our trip, of course."

"What trip?"

"Well, over to Capri. Don't you remember how excitied you were that we'd take a boat there across the Bay of Naples?"

"What?"

Next thing I knew, Oskar came in to me freshly shaven, still in pajamas, and sat down at the edge of my bed to kiss me good morning. I got quite bewildered. What was going on? Did I have a lapse of memory?

When Oskar saw confusion written all over my face, he ordered breakfast to be brought up.

"A good Italian espresso with some milk, as you like it, will wake you up. I must have tired you out completely. But isn't that what honeymoons are meant to be?"

So, we were on our honeymoon in Naples. How exciting. I vaguely remembered now the beautiful ceremony in Vienna and the reception in the Hotel Bristol; all those elegant gowns, the ladies wearing those huge hats that were in vogue. I remembered the endless rows of horse and buggies. Then off we went by train through the Alps, the Brenner Pass on to Milan, Rome, and finally Naples. I recalled now the beautiful setting of this city as I first glimpsed it and the friendly Italians taking us to our hotel on the Posilippo. You had a perfect view from there at the Bay of Naples. We spotted the bulk of Vesuvius to our left. Its stone cape without trees made it somewhat forbidding, reminding one of its treacherous character. As the sun set, the grey stone reflected it in pink and purple shades until it vanished in a blue-blackness. The bay itself was dotted with myriads of tiny lights, fishermen in their boats perhaps, or was it the reflection of the stars from above? I couldn't tell for sure. And it didn't matter. It was beautiful and that was what counted. How did I deserve so much happiness I didn't know. I jumped out of the bed, took a shower, got dressed quickly. We ate our breakfast with a very hearty appetite in our room. The table was set in an alcove by the large window that looked over the bay. The whole picture looked like a dream.

"Is everything well now, my dear wife?"

I smiled at Oskar, got up, and hugged him.

"That's better," he said grinning broadly.

We rushed down to the harbor to find out that there was a considerable delay. If we waited for the boat it would take several hours. Then someone suggested that there was a train to Sorrento, which this time of the year was especially desirable, and from where we could hire a boat and be in Capri in no time. We did just that and we never regretted it. What an understatement. We opened the window in our train compartment and inhaled the unforgettably sweet fragrance of the orange and lemon groves. The trees were in full bloom. It was May, preseason for tourists and prime season for honeymooners. If they often give orange blossoms to brides, this was the *non plus ultra* for a perfect honeymoon ambience. You simply could not describe the perfumed air that pervaded the whole countryside.

Capri loomed on the horizon in a bluish haze. We got there safely. Our rooms were in the Hotel Cesare Augusto; it was perching on the highest place with a fantastic view. We walked all over the island. It had some lovely small homes, villas, flower gardens, fountains, and a few tourists. We were mostly left to ourselves and we enjoyed that. We shopped for some gifts in the tiny curio shops. The next day we went to see the Blue Grotto. It looked more like a stage set for a ballet than something in real life. We admired the *faraglioni*, the odd-shaped rocks by one of the marinas in the deep blue water. White seagulls were circling and diving for fish. It was too cold for swimming.

After a few blissful days we returned to Naples by boat. We wandered around the open markets that were noisy and smelly and full of life. They were also full of skinned animals, fish, and *frutta di mare*.

Some of these were hanging with flies buzzing all over them. It was rather disconcerting, but what they served us on the plates was both appetizing and delicious. We also tasted our very first pizza and found it interesting. Then we decided to stay a few days in Rome.

What a place that is. I have to force myself to skip the descriptions, or else the two-thousand-first book would follow. That many, if not more, had been written about the Eternal City. Just one word. Perhaps the things I liked most besides the *Forum* and the *Colosseum* and *St. Peter's* were the fountains amidst the closed and opened umbrella-shaped *pineas,* so characteristic of that region.

I noticed something about Oskar that I had never seen before. People, especially women, catered to him with such unfeigned attention, what seemed to be—well, how should I put it, adulation. Yes, that's what it was. All right, he was extremely good-looking, virile-looking, and still had a boyish charm. This combination is most attractive to a great variety of women: those who need a roughneck, those who wanted a gentleman; no, it is not a contradiction, only in words, it was there in him all right—and he would appeal also to those who wanted to lavish maternal feelings on their men. He seemed to take it with a simple smile, as if that treatment was the most natural thing in the world. It was for him, evidently. It must have surrounded him all his life, it was part of him, rather an extension of him; as if someone who stepped close enough into his "domain," that person, including men too, but mostly women, fell under his spell, as it were. I seriously doubt that he was aware of it. What one is used to one does not notice anymore. Still, he couldn't have been totally oblivious to it. Perhaps he even counted on it. What am I saying? It is rather that if it had suddenly stopped, he would have not just become aware of it, but he would have felt definitely hurt. It was his due, his charm's due, and that was as much a part of him as any other tangible and visible part, like legs, hands, etc.

The time came to return home to Vienna. We had a charming apartment in the first district in the heart of town close to the *Stephan's Kirche,* the over one-thousand-year-old Gothic cathedral with its lone spire; and it was not far from the Burg, the seat of the Habsburgs. Old *Franz Joseph* was still in there with his tragic, if most illustrious fate. I emphasized the tragedy—after all, he was a man too, even if the emperor of the mighty Austro-Hungarian Empire. I often brooded about the cruel fate that had haunted him. Many hated him outside the empire, but mostly they adored the old man. Those who hated him were either politicians or those he persecuted, again for political reasons. Mother knew the *Vetsera* family whose daughter, Maria, was the one they found shot to death together with Rudolph, the Archduke of Austria, the emperor's only son, heir to the throne. It was an old story, and *Mayerling* was still a subject giving food for a great variety of extreme speculations as to what had really taken place in that remote hunting lodge situated in the midst of the Vienna Woods. No one knew for sure. Most people were still alive who had served there or moved in the circles and gossips never stopped. Perhaps they'd never fade away. Then the beautiful Elizabeth, the emperor's wife, was also shot by an anarchist. All this happened when I was a little girl. And now I was a young bride, married to one of the lesser gentries, if slightly impoverished. The family had a *nimbus*. They came from Hungary, still had some land there, and settled in Vienna. It was often the case that the gentry somewhat hard off in cash married into the rich bourgeoisie. It was an accepted custom and both sides were satisfied. It ensured a life of luxury for the offspring of these old families and gave title and enviable social position to the pampered young ladies of common birth.

Oskar needed something to do, even if only for appearance's sake. Lots of prospects were sorted out and taken into consideration. As it happened, fate presented itself to solve the problem. That summer, barely two months after we returned from our honeymoon, *Francis Ferdinand* and his wife were shot in *Sarajevo,* a remote town in the distant regions of the Empire, somewhere in *Bosnia*. This was another fatal shooting in the life of Francis Joseph. Francis Ferdinand was the emperor's nephew, and the new heir to the throne.

The shot, as they say, was heard around the world; it was considered later as the very first shot of the Great War that broke out shortly afterwards, as a direct result of this assassination. In reality it was only the last drop to add to many, many other causes.

Oskar was instantly recalled into the reserve. He left in good spirits; it almost seemed to me that he was quite relieved that his problem was at least temporarily solved. I am convinced that he liked his saber and uniform more than any kind of work upon which his class always looked down.

He looked dashing in his Hussar's uniform and during the remaining days in Vienna, I was the envy of town, walking at his side or riding with him in an open carriage pulled by his favorite light gray mares. He was very attentive and sweet to me those last few days and promised to come home in one piece if he could help it.

I tossed and turned and opened my eyes in a room I had never seen before. It was all white and there was a strange woman sitting, wearing a nurse's uniform.

"Where am I?" I asked her.

She got up and came to my bedside. "My dear, you're in a sanitarium."

"Whatever for? When did I get here and how? Did I have an accident?"

The phone was ringing; she had to answer it. "Yes, Ma'am, the Miss just woke up and asked questions. Would you like to talk to her?" and she brought the phone over to me.

"Yes, who is it? Ah, Maman, what am I doing here?"

"My darling child, thank God that you are yourself again. We don't know what happened; you were very sick, but it seems you're getting better. I am coming over right away. Wait for me."

"Well, of course I wait, I am in a bed and remember nothing at all about getting here or why and when."

I hung up and started thinking. I preferred to find out from Maman what had happened rather than from that strange nurse. She seemed to be relieved when I didn't ask her any more questions. I closed my eyes again. It was more comfortable and this way I could concentrate on this puzzling situation. For the life of me I could not recall getting there.

Whether I dozed off or not, I am not sure, but suddenly Maman was kissing me and I opened my eyes and hugged her, sitting up in the bed. I felt exhausted and very weak.

"Thank you for coming back to us," said Maman.

"Coming back? From where?" I asked, wondering and by now quite bewildered. "Where have I been?" I asked with eyes wide open and incredulous.

"We don't know." She cleared her throat. "I don't mean you were gone physically, but you were very sick, you had high fever when we returned from the country. We were really angry with Caroline that she undertook to treat you by herself instead of calling us or Dr. Brueck. I still cannot understand it. She meant well, but... At any rate, Dr. Brueck ordered you here instantly and they took tests, but you would not regain your consciousness and mumbled incomprehensible things, often mentioning Oskar and talking to him. It seemed you thought you were in Italy, then again nothing. You must have been delirious."

"Italy?" I gasped. "Oskar?" I felt strongly disturbed suddenly and a fatigue came over me. I fell back on my pillow, my temples throbbing strongly, and I fell asleep again.

I heard voices from the next room talking about Oskar having left. He had to report to his regiment in Budapest. Then somebody was lecturing to someone else about the historical background of the war in a nutshell, in a rather rebellious tone. I was surprised to hear it. I wished I knew who was talking, but for the life of me I could not recognize the man's voice, though I must have known him if he was at Mother's place, where I had stayed since Oskar had left. I tried to get up to go and see, but my legs seemed to weigh me down and I could not lift them no matter how hard I have tried. I heard the voice again:

"Throughout centuries, when only the throne and the altar, the Emperor and the Church were the only powers, the Habsburgs were the strongest support of the Catholic Church, the great power of Europe."

Habsburgs? I wondered. Am I in a history class? Why bring up the past suddenly, when there are more imminent problems at present? Tossing and turning to find out the puzzle, I felt the throbbing in my temples again and the voice in the next room continued:

"The organization of the royal power can be seen in its clearest form in its origin in England. William the Conqueror subjugated England and parceled out the whole country among his military leaders, some hundred barons. To them belonged everything: country and its people. They, the people were obliged in case of war to follow him to levy and equip soldiers; they forced their subjects into that. This took place in the eleventh century and thus feudalism was founded, which flourished for many, many more centuries. It was the case in Hungary and Bohemia where immense estates, parts of the country, were given to army leaders; and huge land properties to the Church. Over time, although they kept the properties, their obligations fell in desuetude. The Emperor was the Defender of the Faith; he eradicated the Reformation with blood and fire. Emperor and Pope were eminences in Europe. The people, the subjects were of no account, they were serfs of the royal counts; these latter were often foreigners whose ancestors had subjugated the people."

I wanted to drown out the voice, it irritated me, but it went on relentlessly and I had to listen, willy-nilly.

"Often they wouldn't even speak the language of the people; in England they spoke French, in Hungary, Latin. The emperor and the high nobility formed a closed body - they were the Reich. Now the French Revolution put an end to the power of the nobility; the people became aware of their own strength, this new power! This new doctrine soon spread over Europe. Nationalities have sprung up, and in its step diverse powers in multilingual Austria that were devoid of rights and bent on obtaining power. This struggle for the victory of this new doctrine is the real cause of the Great War. The nationalities have achieved their goals in a world that went up in fire. The ancient, great Empire of the Habsburgs now lay in ruins; its dynasty lost its throne."

What? I wondered. This man already knows the end of the war and how it turned out? Or is it over and I don't even know what happened? What's going on? Something is completely wrong. I desperately struggled to get out of that bed that seemed to hold me as if I had been its prisoner. I felt that I was drenched in perspiration and knew that someone was wiping my forehead and face with a warm damp cloth and it felt good. I was so thankful. I did not see the person, however, and only heard whispers, completely unintelligible, as there was a droning, muffled sensation in my ears.

I seemed to have lost consciousness and dozed off, heavily lying on my pillow. But if the war was over, didn't Oskar come back to me? Oh yes, I remembered suddenly, I got an avalanche of military postcards, first from Przemysl, where he fell prisoner of war of the Russians while defending this Polish fortress. Then mail came from other parts, *Chabarovsk, Tobolsk,* lately *Vladivostok*. I remembered now how I was checking the map to see where in the world those places were and kept wondering what his life was like. The cards were always sweet, reassuring me that he was fine, was not hungry, and I should keep up my good spirits until we meet again. I liked to believe that all this was true, but when he mentioned that he was not hungry, I somehow became suspicious that perhaps he was, otherwise why would someone mention such a thing? I had never been hungry and in a situation where I could not satisfy it. I could not even think of such a thing. He must be suffering who knows what shortages and deprivations. After all, war is no picnic. What a ridiculous statement.

But if the war was over, as that conversation that I overheard had suggested, how long did it last and why didn't I know about it? What could have happened? Why couldn't I get out of here and go and be with my family? Where were they? Why weren't they with me and why was I not with them? Something told me that I could not get to the bottom of this puzzle. Puzzle? How long ago it was when we used to play those puzzle-games where you were in a maze and had to find your way out with a pencil, but you constantly "ran" against a "wall." That's the way I felt now.

Then suddenly a revelation came to me. Oskar did come back, but he was not the same man he was when he left. Gone was his good nature, his impeccable manners. He became brooding and showed a total lack of interest in everything. Both the family and the doctor reassured me that it was only temporary, a result of the war, it would pass. I wanted a child badly, he refused categorically and from that point on avoided me as if I had the plague. I withdrew from him, rather the other way around, and after a year I decided to live the rest of my life in a convent. No one could talk me out of it. I didn't want any part of this life anymore. I was—bittered by Oskar's betrayal. Others who were with him and were lucky enough to return without a scratch on their body, if not without one on their soul, continued their life and lived happily. Why not Oskar? Mother even suggested I marry someone else, I was still young, etc, etc. I knew that I could never trust another man as long as I lived. Living! Was I still alive, or perhaps I had died and that is why I could not move, open my eyes, utter a sound. But how could my brain and memory still work? Or was this the way death "operated?" Who knows? If I were really dead I could not go back and tell them that I was still thinking and remembering. Was I doomed to this immobilized state of mind? It was terrible. I wished to end it but did not know how. I was tossing and turning, it was a mental agony as well as a physical one. But if I turned, even heard myself groan in a muffled voice, perhaps I was alive. Insane? That must be it. Perhaps I was in an insane asylum and could not reach anyone, nor could they reach me. Was I trying to think logically as I used to once upon a time? But the situation was illogical, so it seemed, judged by my coolest estimation. Terrible, terrible, I began to scream T E R R I B L E!

A hand was on my forehead, and they wiped me again. So, there was someone around me. Who? With the greatest effort I managed to open my eyes and I saw. I saw Maman. She was thin and looked terribly worried.

"My dear, do you recognize me?" she asked.

"But of course," I answered. "Where am I, what happened? Dearest Maman, please get me away from this horrible place. Take me home, please, please. I don't want to stay here. I am living in a constant nightmare."

There, I said it. Perhaps that was the truth and she hugged me and held me tight trying to make sure that I wouldn't relapse into that void of existence full of past horrors.

"Please, don't leave me alone, Maman. Perhaps if you stay with me holding my hand, you could prevent my going back to… I am not sure where. I want to stay with you. Where is Papa?"

"I'll call him. You cannot imagine what it'll mean to him if he hears that you asked for him. I also call Dr. Brueck. Perhaps it would be the best to go home. After all they could not do a thing for you. Whatever they tried seemed to fail."

"Could I drink something, I am terribly parched." Maman rang the bell and ordered a lemonade. It was promptly delivered and I drank the whole tall glass. It refreshed me and I made an effort to sit up. Maman turned the pillow around and that felt cool and good. I groped for her hand and she gave it to me. I held on to it as if for dear life. It was almost a secondary umbilical cord that kept me alive, away from that unnamed condition. I dreaded to return into it. I also forced myself to keep my eyes open and stay in the present surrounding.

"Would you like to talk to me, my darling?" asked Maman.

"I'd like to very much, Maman, but I feel exhausted, perhaps you could talk to me and I'll listen with all my might and will try not to fall asleep and slip away again."

"How lucidly you talk. I think this time you're on your way to recovery."

The door opened very slowly and Papa appeared with Dr. Brueck right behind him. He rushed to me, saw my faint smile and the recognition in my eyes, and hugged me and held me. I never saw tears in his eyes before. Dr. Brueck also came closer. He stroked my hair ever so gently, as he used to when I was a little girl. I knew that touch so well and it felt so good. Being together again with my beloved family and the old faithful doctor felt wonderful.

"May I?" he asked and sat down at the edge of the bed. He looked into my eyes with his little optical gadget, held my pulse, and asked, "How do you feel?"

"Very weak, but happy to be back."

"Back?"

"Yes, back from that nightmare."

"So you think you had a nightmare?"

"What else?"

"Hmm," he looked at me a while. "We don't know, some of the doctors were of the opinion that you had an inflammation of the brain.

Others wondered if something dreadful had happened to you, that you would not talk about and chose to escape. I myself find that ridiculous. I have known you all your life and I don't easily fall for psychological hocus-pocus. But the fact is we don't know what your condition was. I hope it is behind you now and you'll recover completely and fast. You want to, don't you?"

"But of course I want to." I looked at him and continued: "Do you have any doubt? Do you have any idea, how I suffered in that condition. I am a little tired to gather my thoughts, but I would like to describe where I was."

"Where you were? You mean you were not here but somewhere else?"

"I think so; I vaguely remember now certain situations and fragments. Perhaps you give me a pad and I will put down a few catchwords to be sure I could recapture what happened to me. Though I had better forget it, it was so terrible. I really don't want to remember it."

"I don't want to tire her out anymore, but I think it might be a good idea to take her home," Dr. Brueck told my parents. "It'll do her a lot of good to be in her own bed in her own room."

I was home again in body and soul. The old life was almost like a new life now and I savored it to the hilt. No more nightmares, but regular life with my dear parents. There was one tragic aspect to this. Auntie Caroline committed suicide; They only told me that after a while, as I kept asking about her whereabouts. She blamed herself for my troubles for having given me the *dodanella*. She was convinced that it somehow hurt me. I felt very bad about that, but there was nothing we could to to bring her back to life to prove that I was all right after all, that only a bad, very scary experience was behind me.

As a matter of fact, against Dr. Brueck's better judgment and anger, the other physicians insisted upon introducing a young psychiatrist to me, who after having heard of it, was greatly intrigued. He happened to be a very pleasant young man who would come and talk to me and ask questions after I was already in good spirits and had regained the lost *kilos*. He was really a good companion and we could talk about lots of things for hours. After a while he admitted that he liked my company too much and couldn't consider himself a professional any more in my case, as he was supposed to be cool, detached and neutral. He even admitted that he fell in love with me.

"I am terribly sorry," I said to him, "I do like your company very much and like to consider you my friend, but I am already engaged."

His face fell and he bit his lower lip. "I never saw anyone around, you seem to have all the time in the world. If I were engaged, I would most certainly spend a lot of time with my fiancé."

I couldn't help laughing. "You are absolutely right, I would too, except in my case he happens to be abroad at the moment."

"I see, he said in a low voice. Then he looked into my eyes and spoke again: "May we stay friends at least? I kind of got so used to your company and I enjoy it so much. Would you mind? I promise never to bring up the subject again."

"If that's what you want, I like to be with you too."

"Then, there is another thing. Now that I am being deprived of you in a personal sense, I might pick up the pieces again and consider you a 'clinical case,' if a closed one. All I have in mind is to weigh the pros and cons and sum up the findings, with your permission of course, and only if it does not overly excite or in any way displease you."

"Not at all. It seems far away by now. Just tell me one thing, please. Is it really possible that the whole nightmare started on account of the *dodanella* herb as poor auntie thought, and somehow I agree with this idea, or is this to be rejected as unscientific nonsense?"

"No, not at all. I, for one, am of the opinion, now that I have more or less thoroughly acquainted myself with you, that it happened due to an outside force that somehow triggered a, if not chain reaction, some kind of a series of events that you either made up or 'remembered.' The question is which. If the *dodanella* is really a mind-altering chemical in the organic form, it could have affected your nervous system, causing optical and auditory hallucinations that you put in a logical sequence, chronologically arranged. Quite remarkable, all that you have told me. Your subjective perception of these events is extraordinary, when one considers that no such situation was present, objectively speaking. You might have made that up inadvertently of course, and the variety of information you have gathered in your life simply filtered through your consciousness, isolating you at the same time from the real world and the present. In that case the effect of the *dodanella* blinded your eyes, muffled your ears, and practically paralyzed your limbs. All activity was concentrated in your brain in a remote chain of events." He looked at me with a friendly, warm smile, got up, and continued his explanation while walking up and down.

"If I didn't know you better, I would think it was an escape. But in your case this is out of the question. I have never met a better balanced, brighter mind in a woman, if you forgive me. Completely level-headed and an independent thinker. A strong personality who has a happy life. Nothing to escape from here."

"Thank you for the avalanche of praises, but where does that leave us?" I ventured.

"Well, there is another theory, but it is so farfetched that I can hardly bring myself to mention it. I really don't believe it. Still, it reaches a door which is, alas, closed to scientists, theologians, even to philosophers or for that matter anyone who reaches for the stars and wishes to know more than what we can grasp. It is at the outer threshould of our limited knowledge."

"What are you hinting at? I don't follow."

"Of course not, I told you it is more than inconceivable. I am talking of a less than slight possibility that you have lived that life actually and your gene or several of them split open at the *dodanella's* intervention, and started to remember things that didn't really happen to you, as Agi, but the gene that was transmitted to you was part of the person to whom that happened. This gene or genes merely opened up and revealed to you a past as if though it had happened to you."

I was floored. I gaped at him and just stared. I wondered which of us was nuts, or both. Knowing that psychologists dig deep and try to fish in muddled water, I didn't want to hurt his feelings and not finding any words, not wanting to show my utter disbelief, I simply stayed silent.

As I still said nothing, he continued. "Of course this is only a theory that cannot be proved. On the other hand, it cannot be disproved either. I still don't say that that is what happened, I simply state that I don't know; neither does, however, anyone else. I am referring naturally to the two very illustrious collegues who handled your case. They don't even have a theory. I believe it'll be a long time before such findings can be substantiated, if ever. Right now, with the war going on, one simply has to wait and see. But, I for one will never forget this case and will try to pry open this mysterious door that you cracked open slightly. If you did, that is," he added with a smile.

His dark brown eyes shone in his somewhat pale face and he combed through his bushy hair with his bony fingers, as was his custom when he was thinking, or at a loss for more words.

"One more thing, Agi. Could I get some of this *dodanella*? I am not going to take it, just want to see it, so I could get hold of some after the war, so I'll be able to identify it."

I went downstairs and found it easily in the tin box with its double top to secure the tea, or in this case the herb's pungeant aroma. I gave him the whole box. He sniffed at it and made a funny grimace.

When he came the next time, he was visibly ill at ease and kept clearing his throat frequently.

"Is something wrong?" I asked finally, trying to help him to come out with whatever was on his mind.

"No, Just a thought popped into my head that I cannot chase away. Since I did not know that aunt of yours, I mean no disrespect, would there be any chance that she might have put something else into your brew of herbs besides this *dodanella*?"

"What do you have in mind?" The minute I asked this, I realized what he had on his mind. "Oh no, you're not thinking of a poison?"

"No poison, just some other chemical concoction that she might have added to help you. One never knows with older women, especially as she came from that part of Transylvania replete with legends."

"I don't know what she gave me, but she said it was the *dodanella*, and I have no doubt that that was all. I have known her all my life, she raised me and adored me and pampered me. She could only mean well."

"It is not the meaning well I am after, but a possible combination of things that might have triggered what it did, that could not have happened by one item alone. Did you take any medication at the time?"

"Well, as a matter of fact, I did. I was given not only aspirin but codein too."

"That is important to know, whenever I'll be able to go ahead and experiment with it. Right now you remember it. Years from now one's memory might not be accurate enough. I will jot it down in my notes for the future."

With that the case was closed. Dr. G. did not come any more as a doctor, but he called occasionally and asked permission to visit with me once in a while, to which I agreed. He was a rather interesting fellow, if perhaps overly dedicated, which was after all admirable. Just the field was a little alien to me and I could not take it as seriously, as he did. He considered psychiatry a science; I did not. It'd have to develop considerably before, if ever it could be handled strictly as science.

VI.

I had quite a collection of postcards coming from Oskar and I was looking forward to the time we would be together again. Maman had suggested to me not to worry Oskar about my past condition. If I wanted to, I should tell him after the war. He had no doubt too much on his mind and why one more worry? I wasn't particularly keen on talking of it either, more like embarrassed than anything else. And by then it was so far away that I hardly believed it had really taken place. I was only terribly upset by Auntie's suicide. Maman also thought that if that came up we should just tell Oskar she had died.

All that, however, did not even come into focus when Oskar finally came. He was rather upset, although he tried to look and act natural. But I knew him better and once we were alone in my room, I put the question to him:

"What are you hiding? What is so bad that you can't tell me?"

"So, you see through me already?"

He drew me close and kissed me and held me, then sat down in his favorite spot in the windowseat.

"Agi, I have sure information that at this moment the Germans are crossing the border and are marching into Hungary, occupying the country. I could only come in the diplomatic car, otherwise everything is halted. I don't know how much you know, what that means, what they do. I came here not to alarm you or your family, but try to help any way I can."

It was March 18, 1944, a Saturday. Oskar also asked if he could perhaps stay somewhere in the villa, as the hotels would be the first places the Nazis usually quartered their officers in. So the *Gellert* was out, and *Hungaria* and many more for him. He did not wish to mingle with them, diplomatic immunity or not. He did not wish to stay at the embassy either.

"Is anyone home?" he asked

"Yes, both Maman and Papa and the servants."

"Why?"

"I have the feeling that as long as I know, perhaps I should tell your parents. They might be better prepared."

"What do you mean?" I asked.

"Just that. Would it be possible to talk to them in a way to make sure that nobody else accidentally overhears what I am talking about?"

"My goodness, you sound serious."

"It is more so than you know."

"All right, I'll call them up here, this room is more isolated than any other downstairs. You can hear anyone approaching, climbing the steps."

I ran down and asked my parents to come to my room. I must have looked so serious that neither of them asked any question, but dropped the paper and knitting respectively without a word and followed me. The tension Oskar brought must have transmitted itself into me and like an electric current gave them a shock. They greeted Oskar not just cordially but warmly and we all sat down. They both stared at Oskar. They must have suspected that he brought some news and sat visibly tense.

"I just arrived and a feeling told me to let you know that we are being occupied by the German forces. They will reach Budapest by tomorrow. It is possible that there is nothing you can do, "but if there is anything you might wish to take care of before they officially occupy the country, please take care of it. I don't wish to tell anyone else, please keep this information to yourself."

I saw Papa turn white and Maman sat very stiff.

"Thank you, my son," said Papa. "You might just have saved our lives.

Oskar looked at him and almost as a whisper asked: "Free masonry?"

"How did you know?" asked Papa, completely taken aback.

"I didn't know, I just had a hunch, from your way of thinking, from your situation and position in society; from the way you brought up your daughter. No ostentatious jewelry, as a matter of fact, none at all. No furs, that people who can barely afford it get for their daughters to enhance their chances in marrying; her naturalness, no lipstick, modest behavior. All this added up to it."

Papa smiled. "You're a shrewd observer and in this case also a guardian angel."

I asked quite naively: "What is Freemasonry? Wasn't Mozart one? I had no idea that this still existed and that you are a member. Why didn't you ever tell me about it?"

"There isn't much time now to explain all this. Just don't bring up this subject ever, and if asked by anyone, deny any knowledge of it," said Papa.

I nodded gravely.

"With all due respect, you will have to get rid of the emblem." Oskar turned to them again.

"Yes, my son, you're right," and he turned to Maman:

"Let's go up to the attic, that's where I keep it."

They left and came back in a little while with the blue and white leather apron with a hammer and some other tool on it.

"I think you'll have to burn the apron. Burying it in the yard would be seen by the servants and it's too dangerous. A dog might dig it up or who knows what."

We had central heating and the boiler was in the basement; the servants would hear us and find out that we burnt something in secret. That wouldn't do.

"Don't you have a fireplace in the library, I thought I saw one, or is it just decoration?"

"No, it's a real one, just we seldom use it. But we do have some wood there."

All of us proceeded to the library and we closed the door.

"May I take care of it?" asked Oskar.

"By all means, my son," agreed Papa calling him "my son" again. He must have been touched and very much impressed by all this. I could tell by the expression on his face. Oskar took some newspaper. He had a lighter in his pocket, although he was not a smoker. He arranged the few pieces of wood in a neat little pile, put the apron on top, and lit it. It smoked only for a fraction of a second and a red blaze rose to play around the bottom of the "structure," ever so slowly but steadily. If the occasion had not been so grim one could have enjoyed the frolicking flames crackling loud as they reached higher and higher, slowly singeing that dangerous apron, engulfing it eventually. We all stared at it, mesmerized. Papa broke the silence: "Where did you learn how to build such a perfect fire? I have never seen such skill."

"Thank you, sir." Oskar smiled. "We have long, dark winters in Sweden and although we have central heating, we prefer to actually see and feel the fire, to warm body and soul. So as a little boy I watched how the butler made it and learned it from him."

"A man of many surprises," mumbled Papa.

We had to open the windows; the night air was cool and it would air the room out.

"I will clean out the fireplace early morning, just get me something into which to put the cool embers and ashes. There is no need to leave any trace of this for anyone to speculate or tell-tale about."

"It's getting late," Maman said with her practical instinct.

"You said the troops would reach the city by morning. Where are you going to spend the night? Do you have a reservation somewhere? Anyone expecting you?"

"Not really. I came unexpectedly and I already mentioned to Agi that I would prefer not to go to the hotels. The Nazis quarter their officers there almost instantly."

"In that case," Maman interrupted, "you stay in the guest room. It's ready, there is a small bath adjacent to it. Do you have a suitcase with you?"

"Yes a small one, but that's all I need right now. And thank you ever so much. That's a great help on this special night."

"If anyone was helped, it's us. That's the least we can do. And thank you ever so much for all this, Oskar," said Papa calling him by his first name.

"There is something else I just thought about." Papa turned to Oskar again.

"Yes?"

"I'd feel obliged to call my fellows to warn them."

"I expected that you'd think of it, sir, but any such call might result in disaster. I have followed the Germans occupying country after country, in order to help antifascists as much as it was feasible—not many Jews, I am afraid, that was almost impossible. Well, they, the Nazis that is, follow a definite routine. Among their first steps or measures is to ascertain the takeover of the radio stations. They stop all regular broadcasting and play German war songs, Strauss waltzes, or the *Walkuerenritt*, no news. Having this in hand before they arrive they secure their propaganda broadcasts instantly upon taking over. It is just as easy to imagine that they placed people on the telephones to find out what might help them to round up the undesirables fast and without any resistance or help from anyone. Now such a phone call, no matter how disguised, would alert them instantly. One night does not help that much. Tomorrow morning your friends will know it and see the swastika flying high over every public building and the hotels. It'll speak for itself. They'll know what to do."

"So, that's how things are," Father said, his head bent forward, his forehead wrinkled.

Oskar stayed with us the next day, on Sunday. The radio played as he had predicted and by late morning, toward noon, people realized what had taken place. Hungary was the last country occupied by the Germans. Now only Switzerland, Sweden, Portugal, Spain, and Turkey were neutral in Europe.

Days before all this took place, there were some student riots by the *Petőfi* Statue. *Petőfi* was the greatest poet of Hungary, who himself was a freedom fighter in the war of 1848–49, and who lost his life on the battlefield for his country.

Our regent, Admiral Horthy, was in Germany with Hitler—kidnapped or officially invited, you phrased it any way you wanted—and while he was gone the country was occupied. He tried to get out of the war just recently, as he also saw the outcome and wanted to be on the victorious side, but he was not a skillful politician, to put it mildly, and failed in his efforts. He was still the regent when he returned, but the power was in the hands of a series of governments following each other constantly with different prime ministers and cabinet members.

The Nazis gave orders instantly, demanding that their instructions be followed strictly. Jews were a priority item. Not only did they call their leaders together and reassure them of their safety, but they told them to create their own councils to carry out the orders of the Germans. They said if they did so, no harm would come to them. Yes, they needed help in the war in factories and they'd take many away for work. But they should not worry. Those who attended the meeting were impressed by their politeness and "sincerity." The Council was formed and carried out everything asked. The Nazis warned them to pay heed to all orders or they would suffer dire consequences. This of course was understood and a group of naively zealous people carried out whatever was expected of them.

On April 5 people appeared on the streets wearing a ten-centimeter-wide yellow star of David, as it was called, to label the Jews. They could only be out between certain hours of the day, if found before or after the curfew they were taken away and disappeared. They could only travel in the very last section of the streetcar. Once I happened to be in that section of the streetcar and it was crowded with passengers pressed together at the noon hour. I encountered something I will never forget. A man must have perhaps stepped on another's foot, and the one hurt called out loud, "Oaf."

As there was no answer he looked at the "oaf" to see why he kept mum, I watched him and saw that he noticed the star. With a look of great compassion in his eyes and with grim humor he added, "Do not think that I called you an oaf because of *it*," and he pointed at the star. "I'd have called you an oaf—period."

Poor Auntie Caroline's husband was so forlorn he decided to go and stay for a while with his relatives who lived in the country. He took a vacation from his job and left. What we did not know was that he was not a full-blooded Aryan and as soon as he reached his village, they were already putting up the ghetto walls. You could go in, but could not come out anymore. In due time they deported him with the others locked in that ghetto and he never returned. The poor soul. A few cards reached us before he left the country and he thanked Papa for the good life he had while working for him.

When he left we needed someone to take his place to take care of lots of work around the house, the yard. Oskar was helpful. He met many refugees and homeless people in the embassies and he brought us a fairly young couple. He also urged us to take someone in; if there was too much room, the Germans might requisition the place or put in a few soldiers. Papa promptly went and got the old aunt. She was happy to stay with us. She knew we would take care of her and she wouldn't have to worry about getting food or anything else that was becoming increasingly difficult.

Oskar came occasionally; other times he was gone. He moved easily with his diplomatic car and chauffeur. The Germans respected the neutral countries and did not interfere. This gave Oskar and a few others special privileges that they could use to help the unfortunates.

I couldn't just sit home and do nothing, so I asked Oskar to let me do some work. Anything to help resist the Nazi persecutions. Papa agreed to that too, just cautioned me to be prudent.

First I was only given certain papers to type, but then it turned out that the tiny resistance movement needed so-called *couriers* and I was a good choice for that. I ran into Vera too; she was doing the same thing. Kato also came to help out, but she preferred the office work to traveling and moving around.

My first so-called assignment was to find a certain person. It was not a very easy task. I forgot which neutral country's American Embassy forwarded an urgent request to find this young lady, actually a child, and possibly send her to America. Of course this was impossible, since the United States was at war with Germany. But one could perhaps put her into a safe (if there was such a place) home. All I had was the name of the mother and her 1932 address. But in Hungary as in many other countries in Europe, people have to register their residences with the local police. Every district in Budapest had a police headquarters. You had to take the official papers to them to have then stamped and signed. The so-called concierge also had to sign them in the house where you lived. Then both the concierge and the police had a record of every tenant. When you happened to move to another address, you had to fill out a new, different type of form to let the authorities know of your change, giving the old and the new address. This again was kept by both the concierge and the police. And all this was in peacetime, had nothing to do with either the war or the Nazis. This kind of system makes it easy for the authorities to find you, should they wish to, for any kind of reason.

The story was briefly this: A given American gentleman lived in Budapest in that year. He had an extramarital affair with a Jewish girl who bore a child after he already left the country, and returned to the States. This gentleman was terribly upset, as his only child had just passed away and he wanted to have that little child sent to him to hold on to something. He did not keep up the correspondence for fear of losing his wife. But after the tragedy, he admitted it and the wife agreed to adopt that little one and raise it as her own. It was magnanimous of her, he added. He felt such remorse that any child of his would be exposed to Nazi brutality that he said he could not survive that. Please, please do everything possible. It was most tragic. Except we had a lot of people who were facing persecution, torture, death. One didn't know where to begin.

I met several Poles who lived in special camps near Lake Balaton. They had learned how to speak Hungarian, and as we talked with some of them, a few started to trust me after they realized that I was there to help. Some opened up and it was the first time I heard stories of the type that became common knowledge only after the war, about the Holocaust.

I distinctly remember two brothers who had escaped from the Lodz ghetto and lived in the woods on roots and berries alone until they were found and picked up by some partisans who helped them to be smuggled into Hungary, which was still unoccupied at the time. They had a small organization helping whom they could and that was how they lived there. They were young and picked up the Hungarian language in no time. There existed a school type of arrangement to help them adapt to the country. By the time they arrived they had picked up lice and the only clothing they had had to be burnt; their hair was cut very short to make it easier to rub in the burning alcohol that killed the living lice. But to kill the nits took longer. Well, this older boy told me that they were to receive shots against a number of diseases prevalent in wartime. He also said that his little brother was scared to death of the needle, and since they had no more parents, as they had been deported from the ghetto and not heard of since, he felt he had to protect his little brother and be both father and mother to him. So he managed to line up twice, once as himself, the second time as his brother; so the brother got no shots and he was twice immunized.

This was perhaps the only time in my life when the manifestations of laughter and crying presented themselves simultaneously. I almost choked from this and had to bite my lips until they almost bled, to suppress my emotions.

By the way, I ran into them after the war in a Displaced Persons camp. I didn't recognize them as they had shot up—grown considerably. They approached me, as they recognized me. They told me that they were on their way to emigrate to Australia.

I began to feel like a detective, while searching for that little so-called half-American girl. One address led to the next and after a while I was almost giving up on it. Then one day I started talking to a woman in a rather poor neighborhood of the city. Her name was different, but that didn't matter; she might have gotten married or any other change might have taken place.

By that time I was wearing a White Cross armband over my dark blue uniform and the appropriate headgear. It was Oskar's suggestion. People trusted the White Cross, or the Red Cross. They were all charitable organizations attending to the sick, and now to abandoned children. They always acted unselfishly.

So, I moved around with ease without anyone suspecting me of doing something illegal. Illegal! Ha! Legality has sense only if it is within the framework of a just structure, meaning government. If the government is evil and is practicing evil, inhumanity, and arbitrarily deciding who has the right to live and who has not, then every decent person's duty is to fight this government by dissent, by any means feasible to counteract its laws. These are rebellious and dangerous words, as some people, insane or evil themselves, might misuse and misconstrue them in the name of some trumped-up goal. But those times were diabolical and you didn't have to be some kind of political philosopher to know in your heart what was right and what was wrong. "Don't take law and justice in your own hands"—you always hear it. I abide by that a hundred percent. But, as I emphasized, those were very exceptional times, and history and hindsight totally justify these individual actions, the resistance.

It was much better organized in France, or Norway for example. Denmark behaved in an examplary way, including her king. But then they had been occupied at the beginning of the war, while Hungary was the last one and all the time hoped to escape the occupation, by catering to the Nazis. Hungary was literally the breadbasket for the German army, as they themselves pursued solely the production of arms and ammunition.

I never thought much of the various characteristics of nations. Of course everybody thinks of the Italians as opera singers, the French as the best lovers (?), and so on. But I found it most interesting when reading a two-thousand-year-old account regarding the *Teutonic* tribes in Tacitus's *Germania*. He describes them as warriors who enjoy singing war songs and feuding with neighboring countries, taking away what the neighbors grew on their own land, with their toil and diligence, and using all of it for their own purposes. To sow the seed, toil with it, and then harvest it, was not among their favorite pastimes. Let others do this kind of boring work for them.

Well, there I stood with that strange woman before the entrance door asking for Miss X. She looked at me with a not-very-well-disguised surprise.

"Do you know her?" she asked.

"No, I merely have a message for her from an old friend of hers."

"I see."

She waited for what seemed to be a rather long time and I shifted my weight from one foot to the other several times, not wanting to interrupt her evidently conflicting decision about talking to me or not. Finally she spoke. "Why don't you come in, please."

She took me into a stale-smelling hallway and up a flight of steps, and there she opened a door and asked me in. It was surprisingly clean inside, very very simple. She asked me to sit with her by the kitchen table, as someone was sleeping in her room. I obliged. I remembered the nature of my visit and since she said that someone was in the next room, I decided not to talk and be overheard, as this was really confidential.

"What I have to ask you and tell you is not something you would want anyone to overhear, so I guess I cannot talk here."

"I see. It is only my little girl and she is fast asleep."

"If you say so," I agreed. "I couldn't help thinking that perhaps you do know this young lady I was asking you about. Well, do you?" I chanced and waited for the result.

"I do," she admitted.

"Could I meet her?"

"May I ask you what for?"

"I told you it was personal."

"In that case, I admit that it's me."

"How do I know that for sure?" I had to ask her. "I cannot give out the information to anyone else."

"All right." she stood up, went to a drawer, rummaged in it, and pulled out some personal papers and documents to prove who she was. This satisfied me.

"You had a friend from America many years ago who had befriended you. Right?"

"Yes," she answered, barely audibly.

She looked very much surprised; somehow a light stole into her big dark eyes that was not there before; it almost animated her whole countenance, which was not much to look at. She had an unusually large nose and wide lips and her skin looked rather sallow in the yellow light of the naked bulb hanging from the ceiling.

"He has asked after you and would like to know how your little child is. Is she, by the way, in the next room?"

"What a surprise, he still remembers me. Yes, it is his child. He had never seen her, as they departed when I was still expecting." Even her voice had changed; it got somehow softer through the remembrance.

Then a cloud stole over her visage and somewhat embarrassed, she apologized for this poor flat.

"I don't want him to think that I neglected his child, I do the best I can. You see, he left plenty of money for me when he found out what happened and he was very upset that he left me in such a predicament.

He could not tell it at home as it would have wrecked his marriage. I naturally would not have hurt him. I loved him. Anyway," and she gesticulated profusely, showing all signs of being ill at ease, "as I said I had plenty of money to live on. He even bought me a small condominium, two rooms, bath, and a small kitchen, even a balcony in one of those new modern buildings over in Buda. We lived there while the money lasted. I was careful with the money but I did not work while Rozsika was little. Now, that she is in school I returned to my old job, the bookstore Grill, where I am in charge of the English and German books. That is, by the way, where I met Mr. Riley, when he came in to buy something, as he only spoke English. So I helped him with his needs."

"I see, so that is how you met."

She just nodded. She must have felt ashamed, as she volunteered: "You see, I am not a bad girl. I was already going on thirty; nobody ever told me they loved me. I was really not much to look at, as you can see, and I could not hope for any happiness in life. Mr. Riley was my only chance. He admired my knowledge of languages, we could talk of lots of things. He seemed to enjoy my company. I was afraid if I didn't grab it I'd wither away as an old maid."

She wiped a tear from her eyes in self-pity. I wasn't feeling that cheerful myself listening to that confession.

Then she continued her story: "A few months ago some foreigners needed a private place to live in and they happened to inquire at the same bookstore. Again they spoke only English, so they called me out. They wanted to rent the place for eight months and were willing to give a very good price for it. I took them home to show it to them. It suited them perfectly and I immediately went to find a place for this length of time and rather cheaply. This way I can profit by it, and that is why I live here now. Just for a few more months and back we go to our lovely apartment."

She stopped talking and got up from the chair, then she looked at me. "I am so sorry, I got carried away, may I offer you a cup of tea?"

"No, thank you. It is very kind of you but I had rather get on with my business. But may I see the child?"

She went to open the door, and there I saw a light-blond girl, clutching a ragdoll, sleeping peacefully. The breathing was a little noisy. "She has a cold," the mother explained.

We returned to the kitchen. She sat down and looked at me expectantly.

"Mr. Riley would like to have the child brought to him in America. His wife had agreed, as they lost their only child."

"What a future for Rozsika that would be," came the first reaction of the mother wishing her child the best. "But how could I part with her?"

It was only then that I saw the selfishness and cruelty in that. Had she not loved the child, had she been a bad woman, a bad mother, she would have been relieved to get rid of a burden. But this way? I was at a loss what to say, what to do. I didn't expect such a reaction. I just didn't think about it. All I wanted to do was to find her. And now that was not enough anymore.

"You have to wear the yellow star, don't you?" I asked.

"I do, and so does Rozsika."

I got up, there was nothing I could do. I could not act without talking it over in correspondence with Mr. Riley. So I told her that we'd notify Mr. Riley that we found her and Rozsika. I also explained that we could not write to America because of the war, but I promised that I would try to get the message to him somehow, through some neutral country. "Then when the war is over, you could get in touch with him," and I left his address there.

I took my leave. I had to seek further instructions.

I left brooding about cruel individual fates that make life so harsh for so many even in peacetime. What was to happen to them now, one dared not guess. I don't think she was aware of the imminent danger lurking for all yellow-star wearers. She was not alone in the dark about it. Had I not met Oskar, who knew so much, I wouldn't have had any idea or very little of what was going on. It was so hushed up.

One day Oskar suggested that I should attend a nurses' course that was offered, to legitimize my status and the wearing of the uniform. I obliged and in six weeks—it was a rushed course with only the preliminaries—I aced it and was told that I would make an excellent nurse. I was pleased, but hoped the war wasn't going to last long and I would turn to something else. For the time being I was sent to supervise certain White Cross Homes where children lived without parents. They were either lost children, or from the country who happened to be staying in Budapest and something rather happened to the parents or those who accompanied them. There was enough turmoil, and children were the first casualties, so to speak, as they were deprived of their homes and needed shelter, food, and possibly love. There were also a number of children in Hungary coming from the neighboring countries. They might have been refugees; I didn't know. On many of my visits to those homes there were always one or two children, if not more, who came to me and just looked. Some approached me and held out their little hands to hold on to me. Did I perhaps remind them of their mother? Or was I just a mother-substitute? It was heartbreaking.

There was so much work to be done and so few of us; still Oskar insisted that I spend Saturdays and Sundays with my parents and whenever he could get away, he also joined me.

"I watched you, Agi, you put your whole body and soul into the work, which is remarkable, but if you go on like this, you'll burn out in no time and won't be able to help anyone. You have to control it all."

"Look who is talking," I answered, laughing.

"Touché." He smiled.

"I know, you're a man and I am a fragile creature."

"I didn't say it." He grinned.

"You didn't have to." I grinned back.

I didn't mention that in the very first days of the occupation one of the neighboring villas' residents were taken away and German officers and soldiers moved in. These residents were Jews, worms to step on in the eyes of the Nazis. As we heard, the son was kept overnight as they found his big harmonica when searching the place. They made him play all night while they danced with each other and drank till the dawn hours. The whole neighborhood heard their debauchery. What they thought they kept to themselves. The whole country was split into pro- and anti-Nazi sentiments. I am afraid to say that there must have been more pro than not. Well, at any rate the boy was taken in the early morning hours to the detention camp, where his parents spent the night. It was called *Kistarcsa*, and they kept the Jews there like cattle. Soon they were all shipped to various destinations.

We knew that family rather well. The man was the head of a construction company and knew his craft well. He was together with Father in the Great War. They stuck together when escaping at the end and survived a great many hardships. His wife was a famous beauty and he treated her like a goddess. This man had a funny hobby. He had a lot of singing birds in a specially built glass room and he tried to teach them to sing certain melodies that he played on his flute. Some people thought of him as a rather eccentric modern day *Papageno*, out of Mozart's *Magic Flute*, as they often went to the opera and he was well known there for this unique hobby. Others admired him for it and begged to be taken to that place. Others again wondered if he succeeded in teaching a bird to imitate what the bird heard from the flute and not from his mate. I am sorry that I never found out the answer to this. Perhaps my psychiatrist friend might be interested in that.

Speaking of the devil...Dr. G. called up one day. He wanted to meet me but did not wish to come to the house. So I suggested he come to one of the White Cross Homes, where I knew I was going to spend next Monday morning. He was astonished to hear that I worked there, or anywhere for that matter. We met right in front of the home. I spotted him approaching the house and noticed that he wore a white armband.

"Do you mind walking with me like this, or this is too much to ask? I'd understand," and he looked me straight in the eyes.

"No, of course not," I said quickly and sincerely. I felt ill at ease for his embarrassment. Still, he excused himself for a second, disappeared under the entrance of a large house, and returned with the coat turned inside out on his arm. I raised an eyebrow.

"That wasn't necessary, I told you it was all right."

"I know and I appreciate it more than you can guess, but I just realized that I might jeopardize your safety, should a gung-ho hoodlum wish to exercise his 'superiority.'"

"I see your point," I answered.

The white armband had to be worn by the hybrid ones in the forced labor camps. A hybrid one was a mixture of Christian and Jew in a variety of grades. The person was usually baptized at birth, but had either one Jewish parent, or if the parents were Gentiles, the grandparents or at least one of them must have been Jewish. All that was always kept in the official papers, meticulously showing the religion of every person on birth, and marriage certificates; also on the death certificates and of course on the residential entry blanks.

Then Dr. G. started to explain to me why he wanted to see me.

"I came home for a few days furlough from the labor camp and wanted to see you to find out how you are and tell you that I am still around. I am not at a very bad place, but the work is useless. Still it is hard. The place we live in is an old school building, long abandoned, as it leaks when it rains and the facilities to clean oneself are pitiful. So when I can I come home to take a bath and change my clothes and try to feel like a human being. It isn't easy. They don't take one out of the country anymore, as the front is moving rapidly westwards, as you know. But should they try to drive us toward Austria, I would not want to leave Hungary. I feel safer here."

He grinned a sarcastic smile, then he went on:

"I don't know if I shall survive the end of this war that cannot be very far. One doesn't know even in peacetime what one can expect from the future, but in these days, I mean in wartime and especially as one is persecuted, one feels one's destiny constantly hanging over one's head, like Damocles' sword."

I glanced at him and saw that he looked somewhat ill at ease. He stopped talking. We walked a while in silence. I didn't dare offer any consoling words. It would have been totally insincere. I didn't know my future any better than he did. I knew very well that he had more odds against him. Still, one never knew.

Then he broke the silence. "I just wanted to see you once more," he said in a somewhat strained voice.

Now I became embarrassed. I knew that this meant that he still hadn't gotten me out of his system, so to speak. But he did not wish to stress the subject, as he had promised.

"I think you'll be all right," I ventured. "You have it in you to survive, you'll see. You'll be a famous man in your field, I feel it in my bones. I also wish to stay friends with you, as I promised. We'll see each other again."

I said all that real fast, lest I lose courage, but I felt I had to cheer him up, and that was the only way I could think of how. I noticed that his muscles relaxed on his face, and he smiled, if somewhat sadly, but happily.

"Thank you, I shall remember your encouragement and pep talk and will 'replay' it in my memory. It'll never fade away. Thank you." He kissed my hand, slightly hugged me, turned on his heels, and left.

I spent the weekends at home and it seemed a haven, away from all the trouble. It didn't even seem real anymore. I kept wondering if one was a nightmare and the other the truth, or was the nightmare the real thing and I just dreamt of the warm, safe home.

We had to buy lots of things on the black market, as the rations shrank as the war was moving closer to us. The Germans were retreating and the Russians advancing. They denied it over the radio, but the newspaper pictures showed the maps steadily moving westwards, indicating where the latest fights and offensives took place. The breadlines grew and people started to stand in line wherever they saw one, not even knowing what they could get there. A piece of soap became a treasure.

We had ample supplies at home. Father and Mother remembered the shortages during and after the Great War, so they felt like veterans knowing what to expect and how to be ready for it.

Oskar had to leave again, but he promised to get back as soon as possible. I found life empty without him, even if I didn't see too much of him because of the work we both did.

When I was on duty, going from one hospital to the other, from one White Cross home to the next, I met lots of people from all walks of life and they were always full of stories. And the stories were far from pleasant. Rumors might be a better word than stories; the trouble was, however, that rumors were not supposed to be true and it turned out that these overheard rumors were. Like the one about a woman of sixty, who escaped from Slovakia in the company of a younger woman. The older one showed up one day in her brother's apartment in Budapest. They had not been in contact for some time because of the difficulties of communication. They were Jews. She used to live in Budapest, but her husband died and some time later she remarried and moved to Bratislava. After the German occupation of that country the Nazis rounded up all Jews and put them in the wagons, direction: Auschwitz. This woman, however, had a great many friends and one of them got her out with the help of a German officer who took a big sum of money and delivered her. There was no place to go for her, so she decided to return to Budapest, where her brother and family lived in comfort. That was still before the German occupation. These two women crossed the border during the night through woods and rough terrain. Each of them wore two, three dresses on top of each other and they only carried a small bundle. When they were far enough from the border, already in Hungary, they bought train tickets and arrived safely in Budapest. When the older lady rang the doorbell, her sister-in-law hardly recognized her, such was the strain of this escape. They put her to bed after a good hot bath and gave her warm food. A doctor attended to some of the bruises she had suffered when cutting through thick underbrush in order to avoid eyewitnesses to their clandestine escape. It took her some three weeks to recover and regain her normal strength.

She had no papers. That was dangerous. She could not go out. In those days people were often asked for personal papers by the authorities on the street. There were regular raids on the population and it was aimed partially at deserters and mostly against the undesirables.

Air raids became rather frequent. The Americans and the English dropped their bombs. One was supposed to go to the air raid shelter upon the first sound of the wailing sirens. This woman could not go down, as others might have wondered who she was. And there were always those around who immediately sniffed "aliens" and denounced them to the proper authorities. What was safer, to sit out the air raid upstairs or to go into the lion's mouth? Finally she could not stand being cooped up any more and decided to take a walk. Just a walk in the fresh air. Then, on a sudden spur she decided to go and get papers, to legitimize herself as a Slovakian subject, temporarily in Budapest. Well, she was promptly arrested, and put in a building adjacent to a hospital. She managed to give a slip of paper to a nurse, of all people, with her brother's phone number to let them know what had happened to her. When they called up and went to see her, the answer was that she had been put on a train, direction unknown. No more was heard of her.

I mentioned the bombing. It became quite regular; even the time of the day was the same when they came. The Americans had their favorite time; so did the English. The Russians hadn't shown up yet. Damage wasn't too severe at the beginning, at least not within the city, more so at the outskirts where the industry was. But here and there you saw a collapsed house, or several. When an American bomb hit, you could be sure the whole many-storied high building collapsed and buried underneath whoever was in it. I can't say that I was afraid of it, I rather considered it an interruption in our work. Sometimes the detonations were so strong that one felt them in one's chest, even when deep down in the shelter. How often the walls trembled and cracked. So did the ground; windows broke, if there were any left. It was due to the tremendous air pressure the bomb explosion created, so we were told. Often when one emerged from down below after the all-clear sounded, the air was full of dust particles and made breathing a little unpleasant. Other times when the sun shone brightly these dust and debris specks were more visible and created quite an interesting, if abstract image. I still can see the slightly distorted view it created, if I close my eyes and concentrate.

It is not easy to explain it, but somehow from the rubble little children crawled out and were alive, while the adults were dead. One explanation was that the mother or father hovered over the child to protect him or her and that's how. At any rate, those children were also brought to us and enlarged the helpless-children population.

Rations grew smaller and smaller. One of the main task of some of our so-called forces was to go to the country and bring potatoes, beans, (dried ones), winter peas, and lentils. It became a staple diet but it filled the stomach. Once somebody got hold of so-called potato sugar. This is a soap-like substance, it even looks like off-white soap, but has a very peculiar taste and is very sweet and also nourishing. The milk the children and old people got on ration was very little and more often than not, not even available. So we tried to get hold of powdered milk and also powdered eggs. The bread that you could buy with the ration tickets was black and had a muddy consistency. Few could digest it. The coffee the adults drank was *ersatz*, substitute. I am not sure what it was made out of; perhaps a little chicory was mixed in with who knows what. We felt great improvement in our food when someone managed to get sacks of onions. It made everything taste so much better. It also camouflaged the taste of beef suet or oil that always smacked of staleness. Luckily salt was around again. For a while we had saltless food and it was something awful. The onions, by the way created more sensation than if they had been oranges or bananas. Most of the children had never even seen any such luxury. They had totally disappeared at the very beginning of the war. If an apple found its way to the table, there was genuine rejoicing. Once someone was so lucky as to get hold of unrefined, so-called brown sugar. Cooked with some gruel and powdered milk, it became their favorite food. The children cleaned their plates until they shined and licked off whatever stuck to their faces and little fingers.

We also had to think of entertainment. There were very few toys, but little people are rather imaginative and play with anything and each other in such crowded and deprived times. The highlight of the day (besides eating) was the story hour. We had very few books, but all of us remembered fairy tales and from somewhere in the recesses of our consciousness they emerged and got embellished when memory failed. The result was shiny eyes and total silence. Those children drank in what they heard. You could see how they "saw" with their mind's eye what they heard. Proof of this was that they started to act out one or another story. Not all of them did that, but a lot of them and in different homes. They did not copy each other, they didn't even know of the existence of other homes. It must have been a successful escape for them. There must be a deep need in human beings to find something uplifting in life. If it isn't there, they create it.

This isn't the place to bring it up, but I can't help drawing a brief parallel between this and, for example, the fact that Russians love poetry to such extent. Downtrodden as they were, and deprived through czarism and communism, it brought them in contact with a higher, better existence, even if its substance was spun from words and depicted imaginary existence, the same as dreams are made of: yearning and escape, escape and yearning. While under its influence, one is transposed to that never-never land. It is often a better panacea than anything tangible.

Spring, the most beautiful of all seasons, passed and we hardly noticed it. Surely the magnolias bloomed in front of the Hotel Gellért. The cherry tree, a Japanese weeping one, displayed its splendor as usual on a terraced section close to the Promenade, on the lower slope of *Mt. Gellért*. Slowly the crocuses gave way to tulips, the lilacs perfumed the air, and one Sunday that we spent with each other and with my parents in our home, Oskar was left speechless. He looked out the window, stepped out onto our terrace, took one look, and then slowly approached the apparition, as he referred to it later on. There was the *tour de force* of our yard, a purplish-blue wisteria tree in full bloom. It had abundant clusters consisting of tiny individual flowerlets cascading richly in a haphazard manner. It created such a spectacle that no words could give justice to its beauty. He stared at it for some time without uttering a word. Then he returned and told us, "I have once heard somewhere that a weeping willow tree is half a poem and half a tree. Now I wish to add about your wisteria, that it is half a poem and half music."

No one answered. Then as we sat down on the terrace, waiting for some refreshments, Maman turned to Oskar: "I have a private name for this tree."

Oskar looked up expectantly, so she went on: "*Andante Cantabile,* freely after Tchaikovsky."

We knew that she had named the tree thus, but Oskar heard it for the first time and he was so touched that he had to take out his handkerchief and blow his nose. He kept shaking his head and finally he said, "I don't think there exists another family like yours. How lucky I am to have found you all." He stood up and quite spontaneously and unceremoniously kissed Maman's hand.

Maman stroke his hair and said, "We are equally pleased that you had found us."

Such an afternoon in such a surrounding with one's loved ones was an oasis amidst all the horrors. It didn't seem real anymore and I had to repeat to myself that yes, this was real too, and that after the war we shall return to this.

The news reached us that all Jews rounded up and locked into the ghettos from the countryside had been put into cattle cars without food and water and were shipped to concentration camps outside of the country. Some people talked of death camps. One wasn't sure just what that meant.

The bombing became more frequent and considerable damage was seen all over town. As I was busy with some children who had caught bad colds, a strange woman entered the room, after I said "come in" to her knocking. She was holding a little boy with one hand and a little girl with the other. They looked about five and three. They looked at me with wide eyes, never uttering a word.

"Here, my sweet little ones, this lady will take care of you."

I turned to her, wondering who she was and what I had to do with her children. She stretched her hand out to shake mine and introduced herself.

"I came up to Budapest from the country," and she gave the name of a nearby city.

"Last week when they took away the people from the ghetto, these two little ones knocked on our door after dark. We looked out and saw them. They were weeping and trembling. The little boy told me that they were hungry and sleepy. The little girl said nothing, just looked up at us with those big eyes, full of accusation, without knowing what that was or why. The little boy said that he was scared of the men who drove the group and somehow let loose of the hands holding them, got lost, and slowly stayed behind. He held on tight to his little sister's hand and hid behind some bushes. They were very tired, and fell asleep on the ground and when it got dark and they started to feel cold, they woke up, and ours was the first house they found and they simply knocked on it. We immediately understood where they must have come from and would have loved to keep them, but in our small village there are a lot of people who would denounce us and take the children to the next transport and send them after their parents. They might never meet. We heard enough about these transports, just to watch those wagons go by, where people begged for a glass of water or a piece of bread through the barred windows, whenever the train stopped by the fields. Some threw out pieces of papers, notes, addressed to this or that, telling who they were, where they came from, and that they were on their way to doom. Some of the people helped, others just laughed at them. Well, to cut it short, since we could not keep them, someone in the family suggested that I come up to Budapest and place them in a home for lost children. And here they are."

She also handed me two little packages for them full of food. "God bless you little ones and you, Miss," and with that she left.

When we met with Oskar we often compared stories about the people we got in contact with and whom we tried to help. So, when I told him about this latest addition to the Home, he told me his story. We were exchanging our experiences. His latest case was about a lawyer up in Slovakia, who participated in helping whenever possible, going out of his way. For a while he was successful, but not for long. It was from this lawyer, whom Oskar knew well, that he had found out about a family who had been taken from their homes—mother and daughter. The husband had been long deported, as he was Jewish. The local population needed some "fun." They dragged the woman and daughter onto the main square, tied them, and poured gasoline over them, then lit the fire. Their shrieking of delight in witnessing this new kind of execution was not from this world, at least not the way one used to know it. It was hellish, it was like demons had descended to this earth and took over.

Oskar had more information about that same lawyer who had helped many to escape. People found out slowly about his clandestine activities; they denounced him to the occupying German forces. How they dealt with him was something unique. It was wintertime. The wife and daughter were away from home, only the father and son were there. Two German officers came unannounced, arrested them, and took them to the nearby woods. There they tied them up. They only wore the clothes that they had had on in the house, and were not allowed to put on either overcoat, gloves, hat, or anything to protect them against the bitter cold. They were left there alone. By next morning both father and son were frozen to death. Some people from the little town found them and dragged their bodies back for all to see.

These fire and frost rituals were unique, taking place only in Slovakia, as far as we heard. Other parts practiced different mass-methods.

Greed was not missing from the cornucopia of horrors, either. This information also came from Oskar, who spent some time up North. A Jewish couple paid a Christian one handsomely to be hidden in a cellar and be fed during these hard times. They agreed to keep them safe till the end of the war. For a while everything went well. Then the family decided that they had already gotten from the Jew all they could hope for. They wanted to cash in on their "kindness" by denouncing them to the Gestapo. The Gestapo promised money to all who denounced the whereabouts of hidden or hiding undesirables. The couple was promptly executed and thus the family cashed in a second time.

One day I was sent to check upon a little child who allegedly was living in very dire need and perhaps should be transferred to one of the homes. It was in that same poor section of town where I had been only once, when I found that half-American little girl. I thought I'd go and pay a visit to them to see how they were coming along as long as I was in that neighborhood. As I approached the address, I found myself facing a heap of rubble spreading some half a block long, including that house. I walked back and forth to make sure I was at the right house, hoping against hope that I had made a mistake. I had not. I went across the street, trying to find out if they knew these people. I thought, they might not have been home at the time of the attack. Well, there was no one living across either; the house was damaged and unsafe to stay in. The authorities did not have time yet to cordon off the area as unsafe. I could not find out anything.

"Get out of there," I heard someone screaming.

I looked around and only then did I notice that I was there all by myself and a policeman shouted with a small megaphone in front of his mouth, at the distant end of the street, trying to catch my attention. I proceeded in a hurry toward him to see what he wanted.

"Didn't you see the sign, Miss?" and he pointed at one which read: AVOID THIS AREA, FALLING WALLS, DANGER!

"I overlooked it," I admitted, looking at him.

He just shook his head. "Be more careful the next time. It might have cost your life or at least an injury."

There were all kind of rumors again that the deportation would start within days. Then again some government decree postponed it. That went on for a while. One also heard of a man called Adolf Eichmann, who requisitioned a villa in Buda and who according to rumors hated Jews with such a vengeance that though Hitler and Himmler had ordered the wagons to be used for the German soldiers alone, this Nazi disregarded it and went on with stuffing them with Jewish transports, heading out of the country. It was also said that he personally shot a small boy who stole an apple from "his" yard to slake his hunger. He was a little Jewish boy who went hungry after his parents had been taken away and he became homeless, wondering around aimlessly.

Oskar was away again. This time he said he was going to briefly visit his mother. He asked for a photgraph of me to take along, "until you meet in person," he added with a smile and a kiss.

I was without him again and my heart was heavy. Would the country succeed in getting out of the war before all the remaining Jews of Europe were also deported to unknown destination and before the Russians came? The opinions were divided. Everybody speculated while trying to get supplies in case...in case of what? I wondered.

Summer came and went. The routine of my work, the dreadful news about soldiers, conditions in forced labor camps, horrible individual fates circulated and made one wonder what the world was coming to. A few of the Homes were damaged and we had to put the children together into the remaining ones. This resulted in epidemics occasionally. The acquisition of food was getting harder; obtaining medication was also a very big problem. By that time people not only had yellow stars but certain assigned houses too. This took place already in the latter part of spring.

The next time Oskar came, he asked me to change my work at least partially. I was to be occupied in a different line of work. I was to deliver certain special papers to either forced labor camps or other detention camps scattered all over. I would have to travel by train to most places. Oskar insisted I keep my uniform and nurses' papers. He usually did this kind of work himself and by car, but he had to leave again unexpectedly and he thought I could take care of it. I agreed. My parents were a little nervous about it, but they believed in helping. So I went on my first trip.

I had hardly left the railroad station when the sirens started to wail. They ordered us out of the train. There was no building within sight, so they told us to hide in the ditch, next to the railroad, or if we wished, to run even further and "stay put on your stomach, cover your head with your hands." I ran rather far and as the bombing started, you could see it. It was the first time that I witnessed such a scene, as before I was always in a shelter. Well, I peeked out and saw the big silver birds dropping packages and soon you saw the explosions sometimes a fire followed or just smoke. They came closer. I didn't look up anymore, but covered my face and head with my jacket. They must have dropped a bomb really close, as its detonation was shaking us and I thought I'd lose my eardrum. I put my fingers in my ears; it was just in the nick of time, as another even closer detonation shook even the ground. Was doomsday nearing? I don't know how much time passed. I realized I was alone there; the others had not run that far. I heard the all-clear sound finally, and scrambled up, really dirty and frightened. I tried to clean myself a little. Dirt clung to my uniform; I started to walk back toward the train, when I noticed that there were lifeless bodies by the wagons and the train itself was damaged. Others were running up and down screaming for water, doctor. As a nurse, even if I had only very little experience, I felt obliged to go and see those bodies. Perhaps someone was still alive and could be helped. I was right. Most people were alive, just scared stiff, and had only minor injuries. I heard a little later that two elderly people died from heart attacks. I stayed there and bandaged the bleeding wounds caused by minor injuries. They were mostly due to the gravel flying from the tracks with high speed, causing only surface bruises. Others needed help, so I waited with them until they were picked up. We were not very far from Budapest yet. The people could go back to the compartment and they tried to attach the train to a locomotive. It took a while before they could detach the damaged wagons, take them away, and couple together the good ones with the engine. By the time we got back to the station in Budapest, it was hours later. I saw to it that all the injured ones were taken away to hospitals or if they could manage, they went home. One young lady was not hurt badly enough to be taken to the hospital, but she had difficulty walking. I offered to help her to get home and asked where she lived. She looked at me for a while before she answered. It was late evening by then. I thought something must be surely wrong with her, as she fidgeted and would not answer.

"Don't you want me to help you?" I asked finally.

There might have been genuine concern in my voice as she finally pulled herself together, lowered her voice and said, "Yes, I do need help very badly, and I would like it if you could do that for me. But you don't know what is involved."

I understood then. "I think I understand. Don't worry. Are you Jewish?"

"Yes," came the barely audible answer.

"How could you be out then at such an hour?"

"I was to get to my brother, who is in a forced labor camp. I obtained false papers and I am traveling with them. But my home is a house marked with the Star of David. I couldn't possibly get in at this hour without being detected and arrested. They watch those houses, and I have nowhere else to go for the night."

"I see," and I worked out a fast plan.

"I can get you into one of the White Cross Homes for children where I work. I could tell them that you might be working there, as they're very short of help. They would welcome that. Would you be willing to do that?

She just nodded her head.

"Let's go then. Can you walk?"

"I can do anything now that you are helping me. God bless you."

We walked to the closest Home and I took her in. I assigned her to the bed I usually used when staying too late. I left a written note for the people who went to work in the morning and asked them to show to this new worker what to do. I also promised her that I'd be back in the morning.

The following day I took care of the paperwork and she became one of the regulars in that Home. But first I let her go home to her parents to tell them about this job and to get some clothes and other necessities. We stayed in close touch through our work and she turned out to be an excellent choice for this type of position. The children loved her and she loved them. I promised her to take those papers to her brother myself since I had to go in that vicinity anyway, two days later.

I found the brother, though it was not easy. I had to go through a lot of red tape until they let me in.

I took some fresh clothes and also a food parcel to this man and as the sister explained to me, there was a letter within the food parcel, with two addresses where he might go if such time arrived, if hiding became necessary. She explained all that to me in utter confidence, just by simply trusting me. Luckily for her it was not a misplaced confidence. The only trouble was that there was a soldier present, no doubt to spy on us and report back to his superiors. I had to think of some ruse to tell him about this letter and that he ought to read it in private and memorize it and destroy the paper. I asked him to follow me just a few steps to introduce him to someone who was waiting for me outside. Of course there was nobody waiting for me. I got up and on the spur of the moment I turned to this guard with an "aimiable" smile: "You will excuse us for a moment, won't you?"

The soldier obliged miraculously and I think I was more amazed than anyone else that I thought of this and that it worked.

Then I whispered to my new worker's brother the message in the doorway, stepped out for a moment and after looking around I said in a loud, rather disappointed voice, "Oh, I'm afraid I stayed too long and she has left," meaning the imaginary companion. We parted after that and that was that. Mission accomplished.

I have to admit that he was a rather impressive-looking man in spite of his rather shabby outfit. He was most courteous and also pleasant, if surprised beyond words. I also told him about his sister working for the White Cross at such and such address. He was visibly amazed.

"How did that happen? White Cross?"

"I arranged it for her and she likes it."

He just shook his head in disbelief, but with great gratitude in his big dark eyes. He was still shaking his head as I left.

I found out from the sister later on, that the brother had wanted to be a physician above all, but could not get into the university anymore, as there was not just a so-called *numerus clausus*, but *numerus nullus*. This meant that first there were a limited number of Jews admitted, later on none. Still there were exceptions. This same sister had told me that a friend of her brother's got in through the intervention of, of all people, the Pope. Somehow or rather through various channels they arranged it and he was admitted and studied. Right at that moment of course his studies had to be interrupted as he had to go to a forced labor camp. He was hoping to continue after the war. The authorities, however, were not pleased with the Pope's help, and they declared that the next time they accepted a Jew, the recommendation had to come from God himself.

As the bombing became more and more frequent and as the railroad was always a main target, my parents didn't want me to go to the country anymore, so I mostly worked supervising the Children's Homes again. Oskar understood and agreed wholeheartedly. If he needed me again, he would supply a car and a chauffeur. But it didn't come to that.

I became quite good friends with Zsuzsa, the new-fledged nurse. She was a very friendly person; she loved to laugh and was most understanding. She was also well read and witty. I was glad I got acquainted with her and could help her. We managed to pull another bed into the small room that was my small office with an iron bed. Somebody managed to put the two beds one on top of the other, bunk-like. So once in a while I shared this place with Zsuzsa for the night. She went home often to stay with her folks, just as I did.

It was a late summer evening. I missed Oskar more than usual and decided to walk a while in Buda, before turning in. I looked across the Danube, which reflected the color of the sky. An unusual purplish-blue haze enveloped the whole landscape, highlighted by the greenish patina of the Parliament and the *St. Stephan Basilica*. This extraordinary color combination if expressed in music would have resulted in a "marriage" of classical and romantic styles, represented perhaps by Respighi. My eyes wandered left toward the *Margaret Island*; it only showed as an elongated green spot from this distance; none of its lovely flower gardens, statues, ruins of Roman times could be discerned. In this case the old adage was not true, that distance lands enchantment. Or is this adage only valid regarding time?

I woke up from my reverie when a young couple approached; the man, in uniform, was leaning on crutches. At least he returned alive. This sobering sight and thought jolted me completely back to the present.

When I got home I found a few friends of my parents visiting with them. They were discussing the Rumanians' recent lucky coup, that they managed to get out from under the German yoke and freed themselves. They argued that Admiral Horthy could do the same with skillful political maneuvering. I wished for that with all my heart, and to see the end of the war.

Oskar was now often in Budapest, but he was busier than ever. He was meeting with a variety of people and authorities to settle certain things. There was a new movement. This is not the right term for it, but it is hard to give it a proper name. So let me try to describe the events briefly. There was some agreement between the Swedish king, the Red Cross, and all their representatives in Hungary. It had to do with about six hundred people who either had relatives in Sweden or had some business connections, and who happened to be either Jewish or of Jewish origin. That group of people received a protective pass, whereby they were declared Swedish citizens. They could officially remove the star, they could leave the houses marked by it and move back to their old, unmarked homes. They didn't have to hand in their valuables to the authorities for confiscation.

At first nobody knew for sure if this was to be accepted at all. As it turned out, it was. Fully. As soon as the Swiss saw that possibility it also started to issue these provisional papers for the "Swiss-related" people. There were also others who simply worked at these embassies and they also obtained these passes.

Oskar and a few others would go after the wagons that had already left the capital or the nearby towns where the detention camps were. They were mostly filled with people gathered and driven from a variety of forced labor camps in the country. If this rescue group could not get them out before the wagons had left, they would go to the border town and get them out there. Oskar or the others would often single out young people who did not understand when he called out: "Whoever has a Swedish or Swiss pass, even if you lost it, come out."

Or they would tell them, "You up there, I remember you had one. Never mind if you lost it, just come down."

Oskar worked right next to Raoul Wallenberg, the Swede whose sole mission in Budapest was to save as many Jews as was possible. He often risked his life in doing so and he knew no obstacle to do more than was humanly possible. His beautiful big brown eyes were full of humanity and empathy. In time he became a saint for all those whom he helped totally unselfishly.

There were some talks of getting out of the war, but nothing happened. Fall was approaching. September was beautiful, but the news were ugly.

Some people who had escaped from the front or were sent home for furlough or because they had been wounded, told fantastic stories. One heard of mass murders in the Ukraine, of savage actions against the people in forced labor camps as well as against anyone trying to resist them. They even talked of cannibalism, such was the shortage of food and anything else. One simply didn't know what to believe anymore. It was bewildering. In plain terms, one could not imagine such things.

The Germans were retreating in *staccato tempo*, pursued by the Red Army. Instead of the Tsarist anthem they played the "Internationale." Otherwise the cannons sounded the same as they did in 1812, accompanied by modern artillery fire. Russia was devastated now just as well as it was then, but this time the Russians decided to chase the enemy all the way back, in order to destroy their homes too. It wasn't enough just to have them leave.

October came as it always did, simply following its calendrical fate. It gave no sign that it was going to be a different kind of October. It just sneaked up on us on innocent feet, giving no indication at the beginning of what it would bring.

It was on the fifteenth of that month when our Regent, Admiral Nicholas Horthy, read a proclamation on the radio about stepping down from the war and declaring peace in Hungary. His speech was interrupted and for a while the previously played Hungarian music turned into war songs, then back to German military music. That was ominous and foretold the coming events in the language of music. In no time the radio announced that it had been taken over by the *Nyilas* (*Arrowcross*) party, the extreme right, and that Ferenc Szálasi was dictating now. That party consisted of vicious anti Semitic elements and they saw to it instantly that what was not finished by the Germans so far, they'd undertake with full speed, force, and cruelty.

First the ghetto was created. The section, where many Jews lived, was surrounded by a wooden-plank fence with four doors cut into it: North, South, East, and West Gates. At each entry stood Arrowcross men with guns, pistols, and hand grenades stuck in their belts. Some displayed leather whips that they used with glee. Did they learn it from the SS or did they "remember" it from the times of Attila?

The streets turned suddenly colorful. Arrowcross flags were hoisted on many buildings and even lamp posts, and similar armbands were worn by many people, including high-ranking officers. Eventually all Jews, or non-Aryans, had to move into that part of the city. How crowded those ghetto quarters became did not matter to the Arrowcross. The worse, the better. The Jews had to put up with it. Many families shared one kitchen, one bathroom. It had to do. They could not leave the ghetto anymore. You could always get in, but not come out.

Oskar was away again and my parents watched with worry and fear what that extreme party would do in the last moments of the war.

Zsuzsa asked me if she could stay in the Home, instead of moving to the ghetto.

"Of course, just keep your Aryan papers," I told her.

I also suggested that her parents could join us, provided that they had Christian papers for their identity. I didn't know how to get hold of such, but perhaps they would. The mother could be used as a cook and the father could do a lot of work in some of the other Homes. They had to act fast, and once they got the papers I placed them in separate homes, for safety's sake. They agreed.

Soon after the German occupation the Jewish population had to turn in their radios. But before that time most people listened to foreign broadcasts, usually over the shortwave length. Radio Budapest, like the rest of German-occupied Europe, broadcasted only German propaganda. In order to find out what was really going on, one could switch to the BBC in London, also coming in through the shortwaves.

Now the Hungarian and German language broadcasts were jammed by the Germans. The English-language broadcast, however, was not, as very few people knew English in Hungary. Those who did, listened, and they told a few very close friends the real state of affairs. Events of Nazi atrocities and the fates of some Czech and Polish escapees were also aired. There were also a handful of people who had escaped successfully from either a ghetto or a transport on its way to some camp, or a very few from camps, and who told stories that most people refused to believe. They would not listen to such horrors. They considered these men insane.

Many people stated that the German people were one of the most cultured ones, they couldn't possibly do such things. Others were more realistic, tried to stay alive, and did something about it. They did not always succeed, unfortunately. The closer the end of the war was, the more vicious became the persecution. It did not make sense, but it was the truth.

That is, it made sense to those who wanted to have all Jews and oppositions extinguished. They had to hurry as the end of their reign of terror was approaching, due to the rapidly advancing Red Army.

Rounding up people from various detachments of nearby forced labor camps, catching individuals, arresting them, all became routine. They were dragged in groups to, for example, the brick factory at the edge of town. This particular building barely had a roof. It was fall; the rain poured more often than not, making the existence of those in there intolerable. Standing or sitting on the icy floor, pressed together with total strangers. There was no water, no toilets, no food for days. Women, mostly young ones, were often abused, raped; the slightest remark or grimace resulted in being shot mercilessly.

The Arrowcross party, now in their full power, denied officially that they were going to deport these people and others, but in fact they gathered there old people as well as little children. Their story that they were going to take them to work in the war effort was a thinly disguised outright lie. Old people and children could not work in any factory.

Erika, a girl I had gone to school with, managed to escape and reported the situation to the Swedish Embassy.

True to their treachery, the Arrowcrossmen ordered these people into cattle cars with one bucket of water and one empty one for needs. The doors were locked and the unfortunate pariahs were shipped out of the country.

I didn't see Vera for a while; then I found out that her father was taken by the *Gestapo,* interrogated and kept at headquarters on *Mount Svab.* Vera could take food and fresh clothes to him twice a week. Then one day she was simply informed that her father had been taken away into a political camp in *Dachau.*

Already during the summer a number of neutral countries tried to protect the persecuted ones in small numbers. Like the Vatican, El Salvador, Spain, Portugal. The most help came from the Swedish and Swiss legations. The very buildings where these legations were located, scattered all over the city, were getting pretty busy and had to hire more and more people to execute the various newly popped-up needs and chores. Part of the work was carried out in the offices. They issued the protective passports and made lists to verify the numbers if asked. The other urgent problem became where to put the ever-growing number of refugees who showed up in the embassies.

As it is known, by international law the building of an embassy represents its country anywhere in the world. Being in it is considered the same as actually being in the given country. The flag of that nation flew on it, the coat of arms of that country was displayed over the entry, and a large enameled plaquette read: *EX TERRITORIALIS*, meaning that there was no admission to it other than by citizens of the country the embassy represented. This gave the building and everybody in it immunity from either Nazi or Arrowcross intruders. Thus whoever was in it was safe.

People tried to get these protective passports. It meant literally life. The number of people having such passports grew steadily. The passports were being furnished in larger numbers, to rescue as many as possible. Accordingly, the need for additional protected houses was peremptory.

Several additional houses had been acquired for this purpose and the people who had these passports moved in. "Swiss citizens" were in Swiss houses, "Swedish citizens" in Swedish houses and so on. These houses also flew the appropriate flag.

The premises were extremely crowded to begin with and got much more so as time went by. Total strangers, families, or fragments of such shared an apartment with one kitchen and one bathroom. People brought with them only a minimum of clothing and belongings. Many had to get rid of beds and put mattresses on the floor to allow more people. They also decided more often than not to put together their ration cards and cook the same thing for all. Some better organized people assigned certain members, usually women, to do the shopping, as there was less danger for them being caught than there was for males. All this was only possible before the siege started. After that they could only live on what they could save. There were no more shops open, nothing to be found.

One day I received a message from a certain man who stated that he had just managed to return to the capital and was staying in one of the Embassy houses protected by the Swiss flag. He found out that his wife had been deported and his little daughter was in one of the White Cross homes. He didn't know which one. He asked us to locate the girl and bring her to him. I knew her and decided to take her to the father myself. Out of precaution I did not tell her where I was taking her, in case there was a mistaken identity; the last name being a very common one.

I went home that evening and I asked my mother to have a food parcel ready for the little girl and perhaps some for her father, especially sweet stuff, as that was what all the children craved and could not get. I also found a small suitcase for her to put her few belongings into it.

Next morning I picked her up and we went to the glass house on *Vadász* street. I got in with my special papers without difficulty, explaining that I'd leave the little girl there if we found her father. I looked around. The place was so crowded that it was rather hard to move. Someone ushered me into a side room, used as an office, and there we waited. Little Juci sat quietly, looking around, not afraid, as I was with her and she had known me now for quite some time. She was only four years old and one could not explain anything at such an age. I did not want to frighten the poor child. I gave her a little bit of the cookies I had and she was munching on them happily.

People were typing, telephones were ringing, some conversation took place in a hushed tone. A young man was sent to find the father. I would have liked to see the rest of the premises but I had to wait there with the little girl. Then, in about half an hour's time a medium-sized man came in. He wore a suit that did not seem to be his own; it was too large for him. He was rather young, but had dark circles under his eyes and he looked around furtively, then spotting us, he rushed to little Juci and picked her up. She just looked, then said, "Daddy, Daddy, is that you? Where were you so long? Don't you like me anymore that you never came?"

The father just held the little bundle tight and tears were streaming down his cheeks. Finally he put down Juci, produced a handkerchief, blew his nose, and introduced himself.

"I thank you from the bottom of my heart that you took care of my little angel and brought her here. You will leave her with me, won't you?"

"But of course, I am very glad that you can be together. Here is Juci's package, that's all she brought with her" and I handed it over together with the food parcel. "I also got you a little tidbit to make the parting easier. I am very fond of the little one."

He thanked me with a voice that betrayed his emotions and gratitude. I was about to leave, when little Juci looked up and asked me, "Won't you come with us?"

I looked helpless. Then her father spoke: "Perhaps you could walk with us up the flight of steps to my present "home," and he smiled sadly.

Even the staircase was crowded with people coming and going, carrying this or that. Older ones, younger ones, children in the greatest possible disarray. Up in the attic were a multitude of people, some lying on their "beds." Blankets were stretched on the stone floor next to each other, like sardines, and there were more children trying to play and not be too noisy. At the far side by the window was the place where the blanket of Juci's father was. He put her down there, smiling at her: "This is our home for the time being, my little angel. I know it is not as nice as our real home, but with God's help we'll get back there some day. For now, just to be together is what is important."

He kissed the child, who looked around, took it all in, and sat down and asked for more cookies. The father turned to me again: "Thank you once again. Please, give me your name, so I can properly thank you after this is all over."

I gave my name, but added that he did not have to thank me for anything. I expressed my hope that everything would turn out all right, and with that I left, kissing the little one on the top of her golden-brown curls.

This so-called glass house was built of glass blocks, hence its name. It was a glass factory that the owners turned over to be used by the Swiss Embassy. Before leaving, I decided to look around there, after I descended the stairs. I saw a huge room that was used for a kitchen. Women stirred something in several huge cauldrons. I asked what it was and they admitted that it was horsemeat, water, salt, and dry noodles.

"It'll have to do. It is very nourishing," added an older woman.

"How often do the people eat here?" I ventured.

"Don't you stay in here that you have to ask?"

Before I could say anything, another woman answered her: "Don't you see that she is a White Cross nurse? Perhaps this is some sort of an inspection."

Not wishing to get into further conversation, I left, bidding them a good day. I proceeded towards the back where I spotted a large inside court surrounded on the opposite side by smaller buildings. Men were engaged in digging up part of the yard. I asked a woman what it was for. She stared at me as if I had come from the moon.

"The latrine, of course. Haven't you used or tried to use the toilets in the building? Or perhaps you just came in. They are filled up high all surrounded with excrement, one cannot walk there anymore. They stopped functioning a long time ago. Four toilets are not enough for two thousand people."

Having explained all this, she continued her brisk walk to the farthest part and vanished behind a door I hadn't even noticed.

I thought I had seen more than I wanted to see. I went back to the glass building and left through the main entrance, thinking of little Juci, who was together with her father for sure, but in what awful conditions. And this was a desirable place for the poor persecuted ones.

I walked quite absentmindedly, still full of the freshly experienced impressions, not seeing anything around me, until I was accosted by a policeman.

"Miss, don't you see there is a raid, why don't you go in the other direction?" and he motioned toward a side street.

I stopped as if woken from a nightmare, just to be thrown into another one. As I looked toward that raid, I saw that the Arrowcross was dragging half-naked women, beating them on the street in broad daylight. Blood was flowing, they were screaming, while the young Arrowcross grinned and kicked them with gleeful gusto. They seemed to enjoy themselves tremendously.

I turned away and looked at the policeman. He must have read my thoughts as he mumbled half-apologatically, "They are in power." He turned and left. So did I.

I don't remember how long I walked aimlessly, until I found myself quite a distance away, close to the ghetto walls. One of the doors was open and a group of people was being led away, closely guarded by the Arrowcross shouting at the people.

"C'mon, hurry up," and they hit them with rifle butts, or others twirled their whips, then brought them down over the unfortunates' heads and shoulders.

I glimpsed that miserable sight, mostly women and children, some older men. They didn't look in any direction, rather followed each other with downcast eyes. They all looked ashen gray and their expression showed that they knew very well that their doom was imminent.

I felt so sick, my strength weakened, that I decided to go home to my parents, though it was still rather early. I took the streetcar that took me in the direction of the Fifth District, where I was that morning. As we neared Margit bridge, about a hundred-meter distance from it, the streetcar stopped and that instant a tremendeous detonation shook the air. People jumped off to see what happened, as the sirens were not wailing.

Well, in a second the news spread like wildfire. The Margit bridge blew up, its whole middle section hanging into the Danube with streetcars, buses, and pedestrians on it falling into the icy, murky November water. Everybody seemed to have known instantly that it was the Germans who had mined it and found the time ripe for the detonation. Would the other bridges be sprung too? was the question on everybody's mind. Should I go home over one of the other bridges? I did not come to any decision, when a car's brakes screeched and Oskar's voice called: "Agi, Agi!"

I turned, went toward the car. He opened the door and I sat down beside him. "What happened, you look very pale." he observed.

I looked at him. "You don't look that rosy-cheeked either."

"We just got off the bridge and reached the Pest shore when it happened. But for the grace of God, there go I," and he pointed to the Danube.

"I just got off the streetcar right here; it stopped when the detonation shook us. A few minutes' difference and I'd be there too," and I also pointed down toward the indifferently flowing water.

"Thank God, Agi, somebody up there is watching out for us."

"I wonder," I murmured. "That somebody up there must also witness all the horrors going on down here," and I told him about the day's experiences. He listened and nodded his head. He had seen much more of that sort than I had.

"Where to?" he turned to me.

"I was going to go home to gather strength," I admitted.

"Good idea. I could take you if you come along to only one place, where I have to leave some papers, then perhaps I'd also stay with you.

One quiet night, clean bed and bath, would help me too, if that is agreeable with you and your parents, that is."

"Do you have to ask? Of course I go along and then you take me home, and thank you for showing up just at the right moment."

My parents were delighted to see us together. It had been some time since Oskar had torn himself away from his duties. I went upstairs to refresh myself and change completely. It had been the most harrowing day, and I thought if I had something nice on and wash off the grime, I'd feel better at least physically. It helped somewhat, and when I joined the family—and I am including here Oskar too—I found a conspiracy downstairs.

Oskar talked my parents into keeping me home, He explained to them that it was only a matter of time now until the Red Army would take over the capital and I shouldn't be on my own. There might be a battle; no one knew for sure just what would happen. He couldn't look after me as he was still doing his rescue work as long as it was possible to save people from deportation, and local massacre.

In late fall the wretched ones were driven on the Budapest-Vienna Highway on foot in sleet and rain mercilessly, for there were no more trains, or rather cattlecars available. It was occasionally possible to save a soul here and there and take them back to the capital and place them in one of the protected houses.

So Oskar talked of his work and hope for a near end to this war as well as ending all the horror. Neither of us brought up our narrow escape that afternoon.

Finally we agreed that I would stay home, but I wanted to return for a few days to try to get someone else to replace me or at least to help the children with whatever I could, just a little bit longer. They agreed, a few days was fine, and I packed some clothing for myself and toilet articles for that period of time. I also had that beautiful ring with me that Oskar had given me, but I did not wear it on my finger. It would have been most frivolous to display it under those circumstances. So I hung it on my necklace that I always wore, inside my blouse, sweater, dress, whatever I had on. Oskar agreed that this was the prudent thing to do.

Next morning Maman insisted that I take along a food parcel for the days I intended to spend in Pest. I said I couldn't eat it when the others live on that horrible diet.

"Then give it to whoever," she said, "but take it along. Somebody will be happy with it."

So I took it.

VII.

There were a few messages waiting for me at the Home. One was from a stranger who wanted to meet me in order to take his child along with him. The other message was from Kato.

I called the stranger first. He was not there, but I was asked to suggest a time and day that suited me and he would oblige and present himself. I took care of that.

Then I called Kato. She gave me an address and name by which to ask for her and begged me to come and visit her. I understood instantly that she must have gone into hiding with false papers and she needed someone to visit her. I promised to be there the following day.

The stranger came. He wore a military uniform and looked and acted the part. He was extremely good-looking and suave. He wanted to talk to me where he would not be overheard. I suggested the very same office in which we were already. No one was close by, I assured him. He sat down then and started to talk:

"Sister, I just escaped from the forced labor camp. We were driven to the West and I had no intention of leaving the country. I was not alone. A lot of us decided to risk our return as we felt that sure death was awaiting us beyond the border. We saw and heard of plenty of horrors. One of us knew some good people close to *Györ*. We were there in the vicinity of that city when we stayed behind under the cloak of rain and mist in the dismal night. Our friend knew his way around. We found the house and were admitted instantly. It was there where we were given a variety of disguises—mine was this uniform—and we bluffed our way back to Budapest. Here we dispersed, each to follow his own destiny. I had an old buddy who put me up for the night, not longer. He was afraid that someone might get suspicious. I found a way to get into one of the embassies. I would like to take my little boy with me. I won't be able to come out of there, for safety's sake. Could I pick him up now? Or is there any formality we have to go through or talk to anyone else?"

"I can take care of it, and it'll take only a few minutes."

I went to the file cabinet and removed the child's folder. I only asked the father to identify himself. Luckily he had thought of that and gave me his identification. He had it hidden somewhere in his clothes. I suggested that I destroy the file, not to leave any trace of the fact that the little boy had been there at all. This way, should someone get the idea to search for his whereabouts there won't be any trail to follow. He was most thankful.

I turned to him before I left the room. "How did you dare tell me all that? What if I..."

Here he interrupted me: "With all due respect, Sister, what you are doing is charity. You must know where most of these children come from. You wouldn't be here if you sympathized with *them*."

I accepted his explanation.

I went to get little Jani, who came with me from the large room where all of them spent the day with toys and one another. He jumped up to his daddy and started to cry. It was not easy to quiet him down. One could only guess that perhaps the little fellow was afraid to be always with strangers and maybe he felt somehow abandoned. I don't believe that death existed in his mind yet. Anyway, all this suppressed emotion must have surfaced in the form of tears, as a release and a deep gratitude to fate that he was not alone anymore. I know that this is only guessing, but I don't think it to be very far from the truth.

The man had one more request and he apologized for it. "Would it be possible for you to get a taxi and come along with the two of us? I made it so far safely, I don't want to get into the hands of the Arrowcross at the last minute. If this is too much to ask, I would understand," and he looked at me expectantly.

I looked back, I looked at the child, and I reached for my coat. "I'll see if I can order a taxi by phone."

He heaved a sigh and kissed my hands. I don't think he trusted his voice to say "thank you." At the last minute I suggested to not go with the taxi all the way. Who knows what sympathies and connections that taxidriver had, and if he talked, they might trace him and guess the whole story. I also had another idea. We went to another White Cross Home that was closely located to the address he wanted to go to. From there we would simply walk. He accepted the plan gratefully. I was holding the child's hand and the three of us walked together this last mile, so to speak; it was less than a block distance. He asked for my home address and said that he was hoping to express his gratitude after the war. I assured him that this was not necessary; the main thing was to stay alive. I wished him good luck as the two of them disappeared behind the door of safety.

Next I visited Kato. She was there with her mother and some other people I didn't know. She took me into the bedroom, so we could talk. She told me that her father had been taken away and they were hiding there with false papers. They were afraid that it might be suspicious if no one ever visited them; that's why she asked me to come. I didn't stay too long, but I promised to come again. It was hard to look at her, as she had dyed her hair blond. She was a brunette, and somehow this light color did not suit her at all. But it served the purpose.

I decided it was time to visit two other Homes nearby. On my way I encountered a group of unfortunates led and driven by the Arrowcross. I followed them a while from a good distance, discreetly. I wondered where they were being taken. Then I noticed that some of the side streets were barricaded, so no one but the Arrowcross, who guarded them, could go close. A foreboding shook me, and I guessed a horrible truth that was proved right when I heard shots. They must have shot those poor devils into the river, so they wouldn't have to clear the bodies away. I shivered, turned on my heel, and wandered aimlessly for a while. Then on the spur of the moment I stayed close to the river bank, but walked far away from that area where the executions took place. There where I was, one could move freely. No one seemed to know what was going on north of the place. Suddenly I spotted a bulk the river carried; I stared at it. Lo and behold, it was a human, a live one, swimming in the icy waters. He must have survived the shot, or maybe it was a superficial one and the cold water anesthetized the pain. He swam to the shore, and there he collapsed.

I spotted a policeman close by and told him to get a car, a taxi if not an ambulance. Seeing that I was a nurse he obeyed and in no time the poor soul was picked up and taken to the hospital. I knew which one and went in to find out what happened. I managed to talk to him. He was a robust man of about fifty-five in a very weak condition. He gave me his name and address and I promised to get in touch with his family if possible. He died a few hours later from loss of blood and total exhaustion, as I found out the next day when I called the hospital. I could not get to see the family as they lived in the ghetto and there were no phones allowed.

Will all the days be like that from now on? How could those poor *pariahs* take all that? After visiting the two Homes, I returned to the Home where my room was. I found an envelope on my table, addressed to me. I opened it. It was from the man in the military outfit. A brief note read:

> I know you wouldn't have accepted this if I offered it to you and I did not wish to hurt you. Please take the banknotes in the enclosed envelope. You have to understand that I owe you a lot and I can't see any other way to express my gratitude. This does not do justice to what you have done for me and my little boy.
>
> Totally indebted,
> (signature)

I didn't tell Zsuzsa about all the horrors that I saw and witnessed that day. She asked me if I could possibly go and see her mother in another Home, just to stay in touch and hear from each other. I obliged. I had some work there anyway. As I got close to that Home the next morning, something was not quite right-looking. I wasn't sure what, but as I approached, I noticed the entrance door wide open. The white-cross flag was taken down and the woman on duty on the ground floor waved me away. So I didn't enter, but walked beyond the building.

A strange woman joined me and talked to me in a very low voice: "I have seen you here before, Sister, as I live across the street. They took the children away. I am sorry to tell you this. No one dared interfere."

My heart sank. "The Arrowcross?" I asked.

She just nodded.

"When?"

"About an hour ago."

To ask her where to, would have been of no use. How would she know? Not the Danube, for heaven's sake, came the horrible thought to me. They wouldn't do that to children. I decided then to call Oskar to let him know. Or, maybe I had better go to the Embassy myself. He might not be in and this incident had to be reported.

I didn't find Oskar there but someone else, and I gave my report. They were outraged, One woman started to cry uncontrollably.

I left and wondered if any of those little ones would survive this and if so, how it might affect them. It was so terrible to think of it that I almost wished I had a cup of dodanella to drink to get away from the terrible reality. But I had to control myself. I certainly did not want to let Zsuzsa know. Who knows, perhaps her mother managed to get away somehow. I just told her that I had to go to the Embassy and was held up and did not get to it, but would make up for it the next time. It was not very ethical of me to lie. I wasn't sure just how to bring up the subject, when someone called me from below. I went down the steps, and there stood Zsuzsa's mother. I almost grabbed her arm, and ushered her inside in a big hurry, up the stairs into my room. She was breathless.

"I followed the children from a safe distance as they were driven away, and saw that they were taken into the Ghetto."

"How did you get away?" asked Zsuzsa, who entered my room after she heard her mother's voice.

"I happened to be in the basement to get wood for the stove. My coat was on me as it was icy down there. Suddenly I became aware of the commotion outside and peeked through the window, by climbing up on some old boxes to reach it. When I realized what was going on, I sneaked out the side door to the side street and followed them."

There was no time to spare, so I told her to stay put, not move, and I was on my way back to the Embassy to let them know where to look for the children. By the way, most of these children happened to be Catholics; some went to strictly Catholic schools and they said the "Our Father" every evening before going to bed. They fell, however, under the non-Aryan laws of the country and the poor parents who had to wear the star found it safer for the children to stay in a White Cross Home. They had much more chance for survival in there.

The Embassy I notified got in touch with the Embassy of the Vatican. They in turn got in touch with the Minister of the Interior, Police Headquarters, and the Arrowcross Headquarters. Within a few hours the children were released from the Ghetto and were returned to the same Home. Mrs. Forgacs, Zsuzsa's mother also returned, after I informed her of what took place.

This was the first time that the Arrowcross stormed into a more or less protected Home. Someone must have denounced the place as a hiding place for Jews. No one had proof of that, it was simply speculation on their part. They were trigger-happy and lusted for killing.

Off and on an individual escaped successfully and returned to either one of the Embassies or the protected Homes. One escapee was dragged to one of the numerous Arrowcross Headquarters; this one was the *St. Istvan Blvd. #2*. There were more women at the time than men and the torturers focused on them. They whispered that a certain *Pater Kun* was there, who after the women had been tortured and killed committed sexual atrocities on the bodies. As this was new to the Arrowcross, most likely out of curiosity or out of co-sadism, the guards relaxed and did not notice several men escape from the otherwise heavily guarded place. This "attraction" must have been irresistible to them, as never before could anyone escape from that place.

Another eyewitness who escaped from the Danube quai reported that they made the people undress before they lined them up and shot them into the river. Then the Arrowcross nonchalantly collected the loot and left with self-satisfied faces. A couple of days later another woman escaped miraculously, also from the Danube killings. She stated that a few of the Arrowcross tortured the victims before killing them. Just being killed would have seemed merciful to those forsaken ones.

In the meantime the bombing became frequent and more and more houses collapsed all over town. Once visiting in a shelter in a completely strange apartment building—it was the closest I could reach—I overheard a little boy of four, he couldn't have been five yet, I was sure of that, say quite loudly and in an indignant voice: "Those Jews brought all this upon us."

Everybody roared in the shelter. They must have enjoyed the result of the adults' indoctrination.

The next time I had to go to the Embassy, I heard of another terrible event. There was a list with the names of eighty people on it, or was it eighty families, I am not sure. They were either Jewish or just fell under the non-Aryan stigma. They were protected by the Regent, Horthy. He knew them personally and wished to help them. Accordingly they did not have to wear the yellow star, nor did they have to leave their homes. They could go on living securely, without being afraid of the Nazis or the Arrowcross. I knew only one family who was thus excepted. He was a famous photographer; not only Horthy and his family but most aristocrats frequented his studio. So did the famous and also the well-to-do of Budapest. He happened to live only two blocks away from the *Danube-Corso*.

This was an esplanade next to the row of elegant hotels that had their outdoor cafés along this Corso with a view of the river and across from it the beautiful hills of Buda. People would sit there May through

September consuming coffee, ice cream, pastry, or regular meals. If you sat there long enough, you surely spotted actors, opera singers, ballerinas, and writers as well as the people of Budapest all dressed up, chic and smart. It was one of the most fashionable places in the city. Below this Corso, next to the Danube quai and built at a lower level, was a stone wall. Its purpose was to protect the city from an eventual flood. The quai down below also served as a promenade, but cars and bicycles could use it as well. It was dotted all the way with black iron moorings to facilitate the ships' landing. There were several ports on both sides of the Danube where one could embark on either the small boats that just took you up and down within the city (as the *Mouche* does in Paris), or the larger ones that you could take for a pleasant excursion to a variety of lovely places. Next to the lower quai were numerous steps leading down to the water. Fishermen often stood there in the summer and held their rod patiently in hope of a free meal.

It was on that quai on the Buda side, where I once spotted the German army marching south. It turned out they were on their way to invade Yugoslavia. That had taken place years before and I remember that I only saw the top of their heads from the upper quai where I was walking. What I found odd was that they moved without any of the fluctuation that takes place when one walks. It was a continuous, even flow. I got curious and went closer to the edge, leaning over the ornate iron railing. I saw then that they were all on bicycles; hence the even movement.

The photographer I mentioned before who was on this special *Horthy list* had a son about my age. He spoke fluent English and went to the Swedish Embassy for some reason. There he got acqainted with Raoul Wallenberg. This young man had a Leica, among other cameras, and was a most skilled photographer already. He often accompanied Wallenberg and shot pictures for documentation. He often had to hide his camera behind a shawl or use some other ruse. He was most helpful and resourceful. He also had the equipment in his home to develop the negatives and finish the pictures.

One day as he returned home, he found the door ajar, signs of looting, no one there. He finally spotted the sobbing maid, who told him between sighs and moans that his father, mother, and aunt who also lived there, had been taken by the Arrowcross. They had burst into the house, seized them, and driven them to the Danube. While she told him that, their dog, Jimmy came from somewhere and whined pitifully and eerily. Perhaps he had accompanied them and witnessed their end. He licked the son's hands and kept on yowling mournfully.

The son returned instantly to the Embassy to report what had taken place, but it was too late to save anyone by then. Two youngsters somehow escaped. One of them went to the Swedish Embassy and related the merciless executions. He saw that some of the Arrowcross indulged in gauging the victims' eyes with their bare hands, raucously laughing at their misery, and calling those victims abusive names. Then they shot them into the Danube.

As we heard later on, the Arrowcross got hold of the list for the Horthy privileged people. Both the names and addresses were included on it and they promptly saw to it that all of them were rounded up at the same time, so none of them could call a friend with warning. Then they drove them to their doom.

My parents called up; they were anxious for me to get home. So I promised to come the following day. I went out soon after this call and as I walked, I heard a noise. I wasn't sure just what it was. Still, it was not unfamiliar. Suddenly I realized that someone was pulling up the iron shutters in front of a store. Now most stores had been closed for quite some time, as there was no merchandise available anywhere. Fresh food items were the only things available occasionally, like half-rotten potatoes, cabbage, carrots. Eggs, let alone meat, had become a rarity lately. It all depended on the peasant population, who used to come up daily to the capital. The few bakeries that still worked, opened up early morning for only a couple of hours. After the people who had lined up hours before opening bought up all that was available, the stores closed again. To buy any of those items you needed the ration cards besides the money.

The store that opened, as I walked by quite accidentally, was one of the best candy stores in Budapest. They had confectionary that was quite unique, bon-bons, excellent chocolates, cocoa, and much more. There were several such stores all over the city. I stepped in to see what was going on in there. Two people smiled and asked me what I wanted to buy. I was floored and just gaped at them. They laughed at me.

"You mean, you actually sell something?" I asked, totally surprised.

"Yes, the management decided to sell out whatever was left in the store before who knows what would take place."

I looked around. By that time a few more people had entered to try to buy, if possible, something, anything edible. I ended up buying cookies that were baked with butter and coated with very good chocolate on one side. Then I bought fudgelike, individually wrapped candy, as much as I could put into the bag they offered me, and two good-size boxes of excellent cocoa mixed with milk powder and sugar, so all you had to do was mix it with water and heat it.

I couldn't believe my good luck, and rushed back to the Home to leave part of it there; the rest I took along to the other Home. I couldn't divide it further, or nothing would have been left. This way every child could get a few pieces and have a wonderful treat. When I unpacked what I carried, everybody gaped just as I had in the store. I decided to give one piece of each to every adult who worked there. It came out just right. The cocoa found its way to the kitchen and the children had a feast from it for at least a week.

I went over to the Embassy once more to see if per chance Oskar was around. He wasn't. I left him a note telling of my return to my parents the following day. I asked him to call me there.

It wasn't easy to say good-bye to Zsuzsa, but somehow I had a very strong feeling that I was going to see her again. I told her that my parents insisted that I go home and stay with them.

I did not want to take leave of the children. I didn't want to sadden them with another parting. Besides, I planned on visiting them in a while.

I was home again. It was like stepping into another planet. Nothing had changed visibly. But I noticed a cloud over my father's forehead and in the expression of his eyes. He had also heard about some of the terrible things, if not everything, and he wondered how much longer this would last. He also wondered how the Germans would retreat and how, if at all, the Russians would take over everything. They would have liked to have had Oskar around. His presence, his youth, his faith, his confidence, and the enormous help that he gave to those who needed it so badly, gave them a reassuring feeling. I promised them to ask him to come if he could spare a little time.

Oskar called the next day.

"I'm so glad, Agi, that you're finally at home. I would love to come, but I can't right now. It won't be long, though."

I went to my window in the dark room and looked out into the night. It was blackout, complete blackout, and you could see nothing except when you looked up at the sky. There the searchlights were crisscrossing the whole dark dome and each other on the lookout for enemy planes. Once they looked bright, then again hazy, according to the clouds. We were used to this, but in the silence they affected me as dreadful, eerie and menacing. I shivered, closed the window, and pulled down the blackout shade. I went to bed. Before I fell asleep, an idea occurred to me that I could not get rid of. Perhaps I was in a dodanella-nightmare once again, and all the horrible things I experienced and saw were the result of it, and perhaps just in a minute Maman would wipe my forehead and face with a hot wet washcloth and I would open my eyes and everything bad would vanish. Was that possible? I wished it with all my heart. Wasn't there a similarity with an elusive Oskar, even if the circumstances were totally different? But I didn't wish to lose Oskar "again." Still I wanted all the horror to be a figment of a dodanella haze. Wasn't it possible for once to keep Oskar by my side?

I tossed and turned and the next I knew it was morning. I woke up. I had no difficulty moving or opening my eyes; I certainly had no fever, and was all by myself. All of a sudden I remembered the thoughts I fell asleep with and I sadly acknowledged the fact that the nightmare was reality and that there was nothing I could do about it.

I must have gotten so much used to my work that I felt completely lost now with practically nothing to do. I also felt guilt for not helping anymore. On the other hand I owed it to my parents to be with them in these trying times, and also considering the warning Oskar brought up about the advancing Red Army. I couldn't possibly expose my parents to fear and anguish for my whereabouts. So I heaved a sigh and tried to be pleasant. I helped some in the kitchen, which I hadn't done before, and I volunteered to go out searching for food, bread, anything available. There were enough mouths to feed in our household. We had ample supplies stored away. Still one constantly heard of a possibility of fighting in the capital, that the Germans would not retreat, and in such case one already had enough experience to figure out that nothing was going to be available for who knows how long.

The air raids became frequent and regular now. Daily and nightly English and American planes flew over us; in addition the Russians started their attacks. They had only small planes and in order to hit a target they flew rather low and they were extremely noisy. They used mostly incendiary bombs; they didn't seem to have anything heavy.

Considering all these air attacks, everybody spent a few hours several times a day or night in the shelters.

One day as I was on my usual search for food, I managed to get additional lentils. I had barely deposited the treasure in the pantry when Maman heard me and called, "Come, you had a call."

I thought it was Oskar, and ran upstairs to the drawing room. Maman smiled; she read my thoughts.

"It wasn't Oskar, my dear, but Zsuzsa, from the Home. She said that a certain woman was most anxious to get in touch with you again; she is the one you had visited a while ago and whose daughter is called *Rozsika*. She absolutely had to get in touch with you. She would come over but cannot. Could you possibly call Zsuzsa back and give her a time when you'd be there and this woman would come to see you."

She stopped talking, put down the box she was carrying and added: "I have to admit that I tried to explain to Zsuzsa, that we don't want you to go over there now, if she could possibly take care of whatever that lady wanted from you. But Zsuzsa said that she already tried and the woman would not talk to her, she wanted you, and she was so unhappy about your not being there, that it was pitiful."

"For heaven's sake, so she escaped the bombing. She is alive! I wonder where she could have been."

I said all this loud, but more to myself than to Maman; then I explained to her the situation. I couldn't imagine what she would want from me, what I could do for her that Zsuzsa could not. I turned to my mother. "If I called Zsuzsa back now and gave her a time, let's say for tomorrow, would you let me go over once more? I would come back right after I saw that woman."

"Well, I suppose there wouldn't be any harm in that, but what if what she wanted from you would take longer?"

"I don't know what to say, as I don't know what I am up against. Why don't I go and decide after I hear what she wanted. I promise you I'll call you right after I talk to her, so you'd know I was on my way home. Is that all right?"

"Yes, my darling. I think that you should see her if she is so desperate. She must have a good reason. From what you have told me she couldn't have had an easy life. I think you should help her."

"Thank you, Maman. Perhaps I would take along a few items of clothing. Zsuzsa has barely anything and she is about my size. She cannot go back to her home anymore."

Maman kissed me and left the room, and I started to pack a few things I thought would come handy: mostly two-piece outfits, skirts, blouses, sweaters, and some underwear. Maman prepared some food parcels again to take along and Papa agreed too, after Maman had informed him of this.

Now because of the bombing certain sections of the city were already without telephone lines. But luckily we had ours. So had the Home and the Embassy Oskar returned to after each mission of his was accomplished. This way we could communicate.

I went over to Pest rather early next morning. The children gave me such a welcome that I could barely manage to keep my eyes dry and my voice steady. Zsuzsa was delighted to see me and reassured me that the woman was coming a little later on that morning.

I put away the clothes, not telling Zsuzsa that I brought them for her. I didn't know just how to tell it without embarrassing her. Zsuzsa was busy with the children when the woman came with Rozsika. She asked me if she could leave the child with the others to play while we were talking in my room. That was taken care of and there I sat waiting for what she had to say.

I was shocked when I saw this woman. She had aged years since the relatively short time I had seen her. She looked very frail and pale. She apologized for inconveniencing me, but she hoped I would forgive her once I knew the reason. It seemed that even talking was an effort on her part.

"To cut it short," she said, "my boss in the bookstore sent me to his doctor when he realized that my strength was leaving me. I was getting weaker by the day and only with very strong willpower did I go to work. Well, the diagnosis was severe leukemia. I was in the hospital and he and his wife took in Rozsika temporarily. I can't tell you how indebted I am to them. But finally I was released, taking some medication that does not seem to help much. They did not give me more than at most half a year. My problem is, naturally, little Rozsika. I can't leave her with them; it was only on a temporary basis. I also stayed with them, but I can't abuse their hospitality. Besides, it is dangerous. I have no Aryan papers. So far nobody has stopped me to ask for any. Now what I would like to ask you is that you take in Rozsika. I think she would be safe in one of these Homes and after the war I beg you to get in touch with Mr. Riley and get her to America. I told Rozsika that they are very very close relatives and want to bring her up. I promised her to go along if I was all right, but I told her I was sick and was not sure. She cried, but I was firm and explained a lot of things and she finally calmed down and accepted to do as I wished."

She stopped, and looked at me expectantly. I assured her that I was very sorry about her illness, but surely we could take in Rozsika and I promised to get her to America as soon as it was possible. She grabbed my hands and wanted to kiss them; I was flustered with embarrassment.

"Please, don't worry about it, I will take care of it and you don't owe me gratitude or anything. It is the most natural thing. You'd do the same for me if the circumstances were reversed."

She didn't answer, just wiped her eyes with a handkerchief and nodded her head in agreement.

That poor woman, I thought; what some people had to endure in life. But what to do with her? If she had no Aryan papers I could not harbor her anywhere. I hesitated, thinking of a solution. I finally decided to get her into the hospital myself. They would take her with the condition she suffered from. It was a hospital for the poor. It was a horrible place, but it offered her shelter, a bed, food, and care. I took her there immediately and gave both the doctor and the nurse money from the money the "military" man had left for me. I promised to visit her and left. I knew it was a terrible situation, but there was no other choice. She had the alternative to get to the Ghetto, but... No one would look after her and neither Rozsika nor I could go to see her there. I left her with part of the food parcel from home when I took her into the hospital and promised once more to take care of her daughter. I knew she wanted to hear it again.

After I left her in that hospital I could not return to the Home. An air raid attack started and lasted a long time. The house shook and the walls cracked where I was sitting in the shelter. Some people prayed, others just stood ashen-white as if turned to stone.

When it was finally over and we emerged from below, the wind carried burning acrid malodors to our nostrils. It wasn't pleasant to breathe as the air was full of dust particles. People hurried in every direction to get home to find out if they still had a home and if their loved ones were there.

I thought I would call up Oskar once more before going home. I entered a coffee house on the boulevard; it had several telephones in the foyer. I got through and he was in. When he heard my voice, he started to shout. "Agi, Agi, is it really you? Where are you?"

"Of course it's me. Why the surprise?"

Instead of answering he repeated his previous question: "Where are you calling from?"

"I am over here in Pest," I started to say when he interrupted me again, kind of nervously, which was not at all his way.

"But, but weren't you staying home as we agreed with your parents?"

"Yes I was, but someone needed something, I got a call, and with the consent of my parents I came in the early morning and am just about to return now. I just wanted to say hello to you."

"Dear girl. Please, wait for me. I already sent the chauffeur home, but I'll drive myself. It'll take me about ten, fifteen minutes at most.

Stand in the entrance and then I won't have to park, just hop in. All right?"

"Fine, I'll wait."

I decided then to call my parents to tell them that I was delayed and would come home most likely with Oskar, who was going to pick me up. But the phone call did not go through; there was disturbance on the line. I tried again; evidently the lines were damaged. We'd better hurry with Oskar, or they'd be really worried about me with those two big air raids during the day.

I was in the New York Coffee House that was so famous for all the literary giants who had frequented it. Film stars and other celebrities were also regular patrons. Lots of them had their autographed photos or caricatures on display on the walls. I had seen only one other place like that in person, although I had heard of many others. It was the Hotel Sacher's Coffee Shop in Vienna, where a multitude of opera stars, composers, and other illustrious people's pictures are displayed in similar fashion.

I went outside ahead of time, so as not to miss Oskar. He showed up punctually and I sat down next to him. He pulled away from the curb and drove to a side street on the other side of the boulevard. It was only then I noticed that his hands were trembling, I got frightened that something was wrong with him and he would not tell me. Perhaps he experienced something even more awful than what he had seen before, I thought. He parked by the curb and stayed in the car. He pulled me to him and kissed me and hugged me. There was something inexplicably and imperceptibly different than usual. He clung to me like an injured cub would to his mother. I couldn't help thinking of something like that, so different was his attitude, although I couldn't have measured it objectively. My heart sank as I awaited his explanation. I knew I was not going to ask anything. It had to come from him voluntarily, sooner or later.

"Agi, I was over in Buda this morning and before I was on my way to Pest, I decided to go over and see you and your parents just for a few minutes. Then, as you know, the sirens sounded and we were detained quite a long time before we could emerge. It was getting late; still I wanted to see you. I could not drive very close, as some bombs must have fallen in the vicinity. So I continued on foot."

He hugged me again and then just held my hand in his with a firm grip. He went on telling me of this morning's experiences. "I saw ruins in your street and as I was getting closer, I saw that your house was in shambles.

I pulled my hand out of his and stared at him in the dark, barely seeing him. "Do you mean a bomb fell on it?"

"Yes, Agi. It must have been a direct hit. I went close and found total rubble. I called and called your name, your parents, only the wind answered, and I stood and wept and wept and could not leave. A stranger came to me asking if I needed help. I couldn't talk and he left. I went to the heap of broken stones and debris to poke around and called again and again. A policeman came by and asked me if I lived there on if I knew the people who did. I just nodded.

"'Whoever was in there is no more,' he said without much feeling.

"I began to hope that perhaps you and your parents were out somewhere. After all, no one is home all day long. With you, I was right."

And he hugged me, held me close again. I just sat there, limp, barely grasping what had happened. I also began to hope and think that maybe my parents went out to buy something or visit someone nearby. But deep down I knew that they had not planned to, rather they were waiting for my phone call signaling my return, as we had agreed. I even recalled that Maman said they were going to do the washing that day, it had accumulated. I simply couldn't think of them dead. I just saw them the very morning of that day, healthy and well, just a little worried about my unexpected trip. They said they'd feel better once I returned. I really felt guilty about leaving, but I knew I had to, and so did they; that's why they agreed. One does not shrink from duty. It was ingrained in the whole family.

"Do you realize that you escaped only because you went over to help?" asked Oskar.

"I didn't think of it," I said lamely.

Neither of us talked for a while. But there was no silence. Our minds were full of crashing sounds and racing thoughts, trying to trace my parents.

"Isn't it possible that Father or Mother or both were out, in spite of everything?"

"Nothing is impossible, my darling. That section of town is now without telephone too. So if they left home, they would try to get hold of me or the Home. So far I had no messages."

"I can't give up hope yet," I admitted. "I just can't accept this."

We sat quietly for a while without as much as moving.

"Where are you going to spend the night, Agi?"

That was when the truth dawned on me. I had no home anymore. Probably no parents, no one. I sat frozen. Then a sob shook me and I started to shiver and tremble uncontrollably. My tears rolled down my cheeks in streams. I could not stop. I started to mumble to myself, "I have no parents, I have no home."

Oskar just held me like a father holds an injured child, trying to protect it. I remembered then, that I had Oskar and how my had parents loved him and accepted him within the family. That made me feel a little better. I finally pulled myself together and turned to Oskar in that dark car. "Thank you for existing for me. Without you I wouldn't want to live."

He kissed me gently. "Don't ever talk or think like that Agi. There are millions who are alone because of this war. It is the one who is living, who is going to survive this war, who has the duty to tell the younger ones what happened and to make sure it was not going to be repeated. We owe that to the dead."

When he said "dead" I started to sob again. He let me. He was understanding and knew that one has to give way to one's grief. If it piles up inside it does tremendous damage in the long run. When I finally stopped crying I asked him where I should spend the night, if I should return to the Home.

"Why don't you come with me tonight to the Embassy. They have some special room that we could fix up for you next to the one I use when I'm there. You do need a good night's rest and I wouldn't like to leave you alone just now."

I agreed. I realized again how lucky I was to have Oskar.

Oskar sat by me quite a while, once we were in the room where I was going to spend the night. It was dark and I felt his wet cheeks. He must have cried in there for my loss, for my parents whom he had learned to love and respect and with whom he planned on spending a lot of time after the war. I knew that, I felt it. He didn't have to put it into words.

Finally he reminded me that we'd have to get up rather early to empty the room for the employees to work in and we had better try to catch some sleep. He kissed me good-night and retired to his room, next door.

I tried to sleep, but I couldn't help thinking that I should never see my father and Maman again. I should never be able to speak to them. It was simply not possible.

I had that lately recurring thought again, that I must be having a nightmare. *All this was not happening. I shall wake up the next morning in my own bed, in my own room, and have breakfast on the verandah with my parents and the old aunt; I almost forgot about her.* Then I thought of poor Auntie Caroline. Had she stayed alive, she would be dead now and so would her husband, who might be still alive, or not. And the servants and the newly hired young couple? Were they all there under the ruins? It couldn't be. I stuck to the thought that I was having a nightmare and I would have that breakfast with them the morning. This thought must have consoled me, as I fell into a deep sleep.

When I woke up, I didn't know where I was. Everything was strange and I was back again in the white hospital bed waiting for Maman to come and take me away.... No one came and I saw that I was not in a hospital bed. I remembered the reason why I was there. I got ready in a hurry and by the time Oskar knocked on the door, I was dressed and had fixed up the bed.

"Did you catch any sleep?" he asked, with great concern in his voice.

I remembered my last thoughts before falling asleep and I told him that I was hoping I had a nightmare and by morning everything would be back to normal. He kissed me on the forehead. "Agi, I think I should try to send you to my mother for the remainder of the war. What do you think of that?"

"I know you want the best for me, but I couldn't go away from here without you. I wouldn't have a minute peace. Can you understand this?"

"I can," he said in a low voice. "I think I'll take you back to the Home. You have to stay somewhere and I can't think of a better place. You have all those homeless children there to keep you busy. They need you, and Zsuzsa can look after you and call me if needed."

I accepted this.

"Do you think I could go over to see the destruction?" I asked Oskar.

"Do you mean your home, or what is left of it?"

"Yes, that is what I meant."

"Only if you must, Agi. It is a dreadful sight, it would only upset you more and you can't change anything. But after a while we might go over together if you wish it very much."

"Could the rubble be cleaned away at least, could one arrange for a proper burial?"

"I am afraid the answer is no. The city is full of collapsed houses, there simply aren't people around who could do it. It is a task that would be tended to only after the war is over. We'll have more air raids yet and more destruction."

I just hung my head. I knew deep down that I was not the only one who had lost those dearest to them. I can't be favored in any way.

We were all in this together, sharing the fate that destiny doled out to us.

Once back in the Home, Zsuzsa was working harder than ever trying to make up for two, meaning for my share of the work. She was most sympathetic to my sorrow. Then one day when no one was there to overhear us, she said: "You know, Agi, you are now like these children here, without parents and without a home. I will take care of you too, with your permission."

I wiped a tear from my eye, and she immediately came to me to apologize, she did not mean to upset me, she only wanted to say I could count on her. "There is nothing I wouldn't do for you," she added and hugged me.

"Thank you, Zsuzsa, I know you would."

Before falling asleep that evening I thought about what Zsuzsa told me and though I hurt terribly and I had my loss constantly on my mind, I began to feel if not ashamed, very embarrassed. I realized that I felt actually sorry for myself. What about all those children who had been abandoned, who knew no family life, the warmth of a home, the security of it all. Even if they manage to grow up and have a decent life, this basic need could never be replaced in their lives. I told myself I had to be thankful for having grown up within my loving family and having such wonderful memories. But whatever I told myself and reasoned with myself, I ached and I cried again and again and missed them very much. I suffered terribly from the loss of my parents, of our home. How many times have I seen and heard of death, the loss of people. They all had families, loved ones. I always felt very sorry for them. But full comprehension of what it really means only happens when it occurs to you. Then you feel it. I knew then that feelings go much deeper than knowledge can.

It was a good idea of Oskar's to send me back to the Home. I got busy and tried to help those children with whatever I could.

VIII.

One evening after we already put the children to bed and retired for the night, we heard something. We both sat up in our beds.

"What is it?" Zsuzsa asked me.

"I don't know," and I crawled out of the bed and went to the window. I opened it. And there we heard it. Someone talked far away into a loudspeaker, telling the Hungarians to put down their arms; this way they could save their beautiful city.

"If you keep on fighting, we'll destroy Budapest and raze it to the ground. It is your choice. We are at the edge of the city, calling you from the vicinity of the zoo and City Park."

We understood then. The Red Army was already there. The Germans must be fleeing, and anyone who had right-wing affiliations. Hopefully this indicated the end of all those horrible undertakings the Arrowcross indulged in. We were wrong. Utterly wrong. We found out within a few days that a hospital in Buda was broken into; allegedly there were lots of Jewish patients in there. They were all dragged out of their beds, and then in their nightshirts or pajamas and barefoot they were lined up and executed.

Two different Red Cross Children's Homes were also evacuated and the children driven away. No trace of them. Wallenberg with the other Swedes and Swiss protested.

One day Oskar showed up unexpectedly, bringing along a young girl who was trembling, wearing only underwear and then wrapped in a blanket. Her hair was in the greatest disarray. She was frostbitten and needed immediate medical attention.

"Agi, Zsuzsa," called us Oskar, "this girl just escaped and was brought into one of the houses. I took her into the car and brought her here. She told me with teeth chattering that she was dragged down from one of the Swedish protected houses with her parents and other tenants to the Danube. The Arrowcross didn't even wait till darkness sat in."

As Oskar told all this to us, we put the poor girl to bed, took her damp underwear off, put a dry robe on her, and covered her with everything we had. There was no more heating. The children were only fairly warm in the one room because it was so crowded that body heat warmed it and we made them exercise a lot as they could never get outdoors.

Oskar had a bottle of rum in his overcoat pocket and he made the girl swallow some, to warm her faster. She mumbled a faint "thank you." She was still shivering, but seemed to calm down somewhat. Then Oskar told us that this girl saw her parents being shot into the Danube together with many other people. Then, all of a sudden—perhaps the rum warmed her up a little—this unfortunate girl started to mumble something, more to herself, than to us: "I don't even know why I escaped. I guess it was instinct, and also because I am a professional swimmer and water is part of my element. Also, the water offered more protection even in its half-frozen state than the shore."

We noticed that she turned toward the wall and fell asleep.

Oskar told us more of the pitiful condition everywhere. He never mentioned the flying shells and shrapnel on the street. He didn't have time to think about that. It was a dismal foggy day. Dampness penetrated into one's bones. Even with the windows closed we heard the thunder and sporadic rumble of the artillery fire, sudden detonation from close by and from farther away.

Oskar had hardly left us to continue his rescue work when they called me to the telephone. It was the *Rokus* Hospital. The doctor I talked to when taking in Rozsika's mother, called. He said that the poor woman was close to the end and asked to see me and if possible her daughter.

Zsuzsa was very worried that I would go out with all the shooting going on, but I said it was my duty. However, I declined to expose little Rozsika to the "trip." Not so much of fear for her life, but rather to expose her to see her mother in such a pitiful condition. Why shouldn't she rather remember her mother the way she used to be? Why add this last dreadful and most painful scene? I didn't know if I had the right to deprive either of them of this meeting, but there was no time to ponder about ethics.

I was surprised at how abandoned the streets were. People must have had more sense than I had to venture out in such circumstances. I finally arrived and saw the yellowish paint of the hospital's walls. I went in, wearing the White Cross uniform. No one raised any question about why I was there, what I was doing. I went from one shock to the next. I don't believe I am capable of describing what I found there. Not just the hospital wards, but all the corridors and hallways were literally packed with what seemed to be corpses rotting away, except they were moaning and some of them slightly moving. All the beds were full of patients and in addition there were cots all over the floors with more sick and helpless people. The stench was unbearable. An army of doctors and nurses couldn't possibly take care of them. And there were only a handful of professionals available, running out of medications, cotton, gauze, chloroform, and iodine. It was the doctor who told me that, but even without this information the picture spoke for itself.

He led me to a bed. At least she was in a bed. I would have never recognized her. She had shrunk to almost child size, with the face of a shrivelled octogenarian. Only her eyes were still—not shiny, but a glimpse of light was in them and that of recognition. She talked in a very low voice. I had to go near to catch her words,

"Thank you for coming. Is Rozsika with you?"

"No, but she is fine, but I did not want to expose her to the shootings going on outside. It's too dangerous."

"I just wanted to see you and ask you once more to keep our agreement. You will see to it that she gets to America, to her father, won't you?

"I promise I will take care of everything possible as soon as the war is over. In the meantime she is with me among many homeless children and she is adjusting rather well."

She tried to smile. It was pitiful. Tears streamed down her cheeks. Then she whispered, "Thank you again," and she turned to the wall.

Two days later I had a call from her doctor. He let me know that the poor soul had passed away in her sleep. I did not tell Rozsika about it yet. I decided to tell her only after I had contacted Mr. Riley and started the procedure of her emigration. For the time being we had to make sure that we lived to see the end of the war.

But I have to go back and tell about the incident after I left the hospital. When I went out the door of that inferno, another one awaited me outside. The artillery fire was on the *crescendo*. Shots literally coming from every direction in a staccato punctuated the pandemonium. Highlighting all this were the whistling incendiary bombs that the Russian *"rata-s"* (light airplanes) littered the streets with. I was so stunned by it all that I just stood there as if rooted to the ground, until out of nowhere someone grabbed me and dragged me to a nearby shelter. Only when inside did I look at my abductor or rescuer.

"Well, Mr. Gabor, I didn't realize it was you."

He laughed. "Miss Agi, what are you doing standing outside in this bullet rain?"

"I have just come from the hospital and did not realize how serious the situation was. How are Greti and the baby?"

"They're fine. I sent them home to the country while this is going on here. You shouldn't be out either. I'm sure your parents have no idea that you're out on the street not caring for your safety."

I must have turned pale, as he looked at me, concerned. "Something wrong?" he asked.

I looked beyond him, and said in a very low voice, "My parents were victims of an air raid. The whole house collapsed on them." I was surprised that I could say it.

This policeman, Mr. Gabor, as we called him, had married a maid, Greti, who had served my grandparents for a great number of years before she got married. She loved my grandparents, who treated her very well and even sent her a beautiful gift when she got married. She took her fiancé, this Mr. Gabor, and introduced him to them. When my grandparents died they came to the funeral. I hadn't seen them since.

"I cannot tell you how terrible I feel about that, Miss," he said. "May I ask you where you're living now?"

"Sure. I am, as you see, a nurse and work in a White Cross Children's Home."

"That isn't too safe," he said. "You must have heard that some of the Red Cross Homes have been raided. Why don't I find you some safer place, would you let me look?"

"I thank you very much, but I have obligations to those children. I wouldn't leave them alone, come what may."

"I see. But give me the address at least, perhaps I could keep an eye on it and protect it or get help, should the Arrowcross attempt atrocities against it."

I did just that and thanked him profusely. Then he insisted on accompanying me on the way back after the battle subsided somewhat and it was, if not safe, at least safer to go out. He asked for permission to come up with me. He must have wanted to to see my present place. He was in for a surprise, having known where I used to live. He just shook his head half-bewildered, half-incredulous. I could see how he pondered over the vicissitudes of fate. He was visibly shaken that we had no heat in the Home and he promised me to get wood for the stove. He kept his word and sent over a young guy with a good supply. I didn't know how to thank him.

"You don't have to. I'm glad I ran into you and could be of some service." Then as he was about to leave, he turned to me once more: "I don't have a telephone, but I will come as often as feasible to check around here. You will let me call on you occasionally to see if you need something I might be able to get for you."

I was touched by his solicitude and said thank you to him in the deepest sense of this often-abused expression of gratitude.

Oskar took care of further negotiations. While Wallenberg went to rescue people at certain places, others had been surrounded at other locations and driven by the ferocious persecutors. On such occasions Oskar rushed there to negotiate and try to save as many people as possible. They both risked their lives as these extreme right-wing elements lost their patience with those rescuers and were about to finish them off with the rest of the "worms."

Oskar managed to come over occasionally to see how I was coming along. He never stayed long as he was on his way to do this, or that.

Going out was also getting riskier and riskier. I begged him to stay indoors. He just laughed away this kind of danger, in light of those that he had witnessed day in and day out for the last few months.

Mr. Gabor showed up again. He wanted to talk to me and they let him in.

"I don't mean to make a nuisance of myself, Miss, but I had an idea. I have known your grandparents and I have never known finer people. Now that you are alone, a chip off the old block so to speak, I can't just stand by idle and let you expose yourself to this increasingly fierce battle. By the way, I just found out that the Russians are fighting in the streets of Budapest already and they are advancing very, very slowly. The resistance is strong."

"Who is resisting so?" I asked. "Do the people want the city destroyed, as they promised a while back?"

"No, Miss. We do realize that they'd come anyway, but the Germans are trapped within the city. We heard news that the Russians are already in Vienna, they simply bypassed Budapest, not knowing how much resistance to expect here. They are in a hurry and want to get to Berlin as soon as possible. So the fighting is going on from kitchen to bathroom, almost. But they are getting closer, even if it takes a while. But why I came again, is this. I wish to protect you from what is likely to come and offer you to go to my village. Greti would have room for you for sure. Why don't you wait there for the end of the war?"

"I don't really know how to express my thanks for your care. You hardly know me. It is touching. And if Grandfather and Grandmother know about your care, up there," and I looked toward the sky, "I am sure they are touched too."

He didn't laugh at me. On the contrary, his face was very solemn.

"I tell you Mr. Gabor. I do have two reasons why I have to stay in Budapest."

"Yes?" He looked at me, awaiting my explanation.

"Well, I have a fiancé here and I don't want to go without him. The second reason is a little girl whose mother just passed away and I promised her to take care of this little girl and see to it that she get to her father after the war. He is living in America. I can't abandon her."

"That could be helped. We could place you, all three of you; if not in the same house, somewhere, I am sure of it. By the way, where is your fiance and what is he doing?"

I told him briefly that Oskar was in the diplomatic service and that he was Swedish.

"Do you mean one of those protected Swedes?" he asked, with great worry written on his face.

"No, he was born in Sweden and is living there. He is only here to help."

"Is his name Wallenberg?" he interrupted me.

"So you heard of Wallenberg too."

"Everybody did."

"Well, it isn't Wallenberg, just another Swede."

"I see. Would he be in the Embassy or where is his office? I might be able to offer my help to him."

"That would be wonderful; if you wish I will give you the address, phone. No, don't talk over the phone. It's better to meet him in person."

"Yes, absolutely. I'll talk to him." And with that he left.

Little Rozsika was an exceptionally good and bright child. She proved it more than once. One evening as we were ready to retire with Zsuzsa, a knock was heard on the door.

"Come in," we said.

There stood Rozsika, telling us that little Piri was acting strange while asleep. We went to see, and she was tossing and turning and moaning. We touched her forehead; it was very hot. We took her temperature; it was rather high. Unfortunately we had no place where we could have separated her from the others. So we wiped her with alcohol-soaked rags and gave her some aspirin for the time being. We were ardently hoping that it was not something either contagious or severe. Rozsika watched us all the time and even asked if she could help us with something.

"You are a very good little girl and you have already helped us and Piri very much by coming to us and telling us about it. This way she'd be better by the morrow. Did your mother ever tell you what a good little girl you are?"

"Yes, she told me that a lot. I'd like to see her again. Why doesn't she come?"

I kissed her. "She is rather sick in the hospital and going out is very dangerous. We'll have to wait till the end of the war. It won't last much longer now, we hope."

She accepted that and crawled back to her bed.

The girl who swam out of the Danube was recuperating and she started to help out. It kept her mind off the terrible fate her parents shared with so many others and that she had barely escaped. She didn't talk much, just buried herself in work, never complaining when the washing, for example, had to be done and in cold water. We used what wood we got for heating rather than washing. Our supplies were going fast now and we could not buy anything anymore. Stores had been long closed and the farmers did not venture into the capital from the vicinity with fresh produce. So we had to ration what we had. For breakfast we had one bowl of either hot ersatz tea with a small piece of bread, or some gruel cooked in hot water, sweetened with very little brown sugar. The midday meal had to be skipped and instead we ate around four in the afternoon a one-dish meal that consisted of either dried beans, lentils, or winter peas. That was the staple, by the way, throughout the whole city as we found out later on. Bread was baked once a week; it was dark, gritty, and soggy and not enough. It was brought to us from other Homes where they had the facility. Or did it come from a baker still working? I never really found out for sure. We all began to feel hunger pains, but keeping busy helped us not to think of it. I also noticed that as time passed, we slowly got used to eating less. Perhaps our stomachs shrank. I don't know if that is possible or not, it was merely an impression. I have to admit that occasionally before falling asleep I had a constantly recurring wish: to have a slice of rye bread with butter and sliced hard-boiled eggs and a little salt. It was something completely unobtainable and most desirable. Why I yearned for this, I wouldn't know. Is it possible that my system needed what that contained? Or was it just a childish whim? I could have dreamt, after all, of fancy meats, desserts I was so fond of....

I thought I ought to visit Kato once again, but surely she wouldn't expect me in such adverse conditions. Only those people ventured out who absolutely had to. Oskar also made me promise to stay indoors. Even Mr. Gabor warned me. I just worried about Oskar constantly. I wished I had the power to make him stay inside. But I knew that nobody could. He did what he believed in doing.

Several days after Mr. Gabor visited me, Oskar showed up. I was so happy to see him, I could hardly hold back my tears from sheer happiness. He was touched for seeing me so worried about him.

"Agi, Mr. Gabor visited me. He is a very nice man and most useful. He also has a good point about sending you to his wife. How about it?"

"Oskar, whether it is *Budaörs* or *Stockholm*, I won't go unless you also come along.

"You drive a hard bargain, young lady. I was afraid you'd say this."

"Well, are you coming, or do we stay?"

"We stay a little bit longer, then we'll see."

I looked at him. "Can you still manage to save people?"

"It is getting harder and harder, but Wallenberg often succeeds in renegotiating in hopeless conditions. When the terrible atrocities take place, one or another would-be victim manages to escape and let us know, so we go with lists and save at least a few from sure death. These are the last minutes—so to speak—of the war in Budapest, so we have to do everything possible. As you might have already heard the fighting is going on within Budapest, but the advance is very slow due to the resistance. I wonder how much will remain from the city. The uselessness of it all! And the price both in human lives and the wrecking of a beautiful city. And we are witnessing only one single city. Think of it Agi, all the cities and countries the Nazis ran over share this fate now."

He sat a while speechless, then took his coat, made me promise to stay indoors, and left with a kiss and a hug and a smile. He returned from the door once more, as if to make up for his gloomy mood, saying, "We'll have better times again," and he was gone.

I shuddered for a minute and felt very uncomfortable. Was I coming down with something? I didn't think so. I had a pretty rugged constitution and was not at all prone to colds, headaches, and other minor illnesses.

This time I was afraid that those better times Oskar referred to were far, far away. Why did I think that, when he himself said that the end was near. I knew that once the Russians took over, the shooting would stop. Still that accursed dodanella dream worked itself again into the threshold of my consiousness and the scepter of the past hung over me menacingly. Oskar once loved me and left me. But that was only a nightmare. Why, oh why am I repeatedly reminded of it, again and again?

The loss of my parents and home was such a blow that I could not even really face it yet. I felt that once the extreme circumstances of the war would be over, only then would I realize how alone I was in the world. Just as Zsuzsa had pointed out; as those homeless orphans were. Of course I was grown up, but my loss was tremendous. I do know that few people had parents like I had and a home so special. With Oskar we could recreate it slowly. But somehow I feared that even after the war his work might come first. He told me how they were talking with Wallenberg of this problem facing them after the war was over. All those who would survive these horrible times would end up with their lives but not much more. They would need homes, food, clothing. The hardest task was going to be to care for the children standing all alone in this hostile and harsh world. Of course I shared the idea of helping. All I wanted was a small place for me in his life.

The noise coming from outside was getting so intense that we knew they must be getting really close. We tried to find some wood to fit the windows in case the glass would break. The first such precaution was to keep the wooden shutters down even during the day. That caused darkness within and a most unfriendly atmosphere. We had to count on the electricity being cut off too. We had some old-fashioned kerosene lamps prepared. I don't know who thought of it first and how they got into the house, but there they were. We had some candles too, but we were afraid of fire with so many children around.

I didn't remember such a cold winter ever. Snow fell, then the wind picked up and rattled those lowered shutters. One only heard them as they were so close, otherwise the outside din would have drowned it out. Somehow that little extra noise started to get on our nerves. It also occurred to me that perhaps it was not colder and damper than usual at this time of the year, just that I used to live in a well-heated and comfortable house, well fed and with not a care in the world. Then I thought of Rozsika's mother. The poor soul. What a miserable existence she had all her life and how many people lived like that all the time. All right, I argued with myself, so I was still young, I haven't experienced too much yet, but what I have seen the last year or so opened my eyes to the most dreadful things that can befall people, and at the same time I also realized that even without such exceptional times life was perhaps more often than not very very difficult, with insurmountable problems. Was it an eternal fight? For some, for sure. Or for all, and mine was just starting? Even if so, I thought of how wonderful I had had it until then. Some never experience such bliss and never enter Arcadia. I have been there. Perhaps I have to keep it in my memory now and put up with whatever was awaiting me. I still had Oskar, after all. It might be just the fear of losing him too, that made me so jittery. On this "note" I fell asleep.

Zsuzsa was marvelous with her stories. She made one up about the sun and the clouds starting a war against each other. The clouds were victorious and blotted out the sun completely; that was the reason we had to sit in the dark. But the sun had a trick or two up its sleeves and was secretly working on warming the clouds up, making them evaporate, and showing her shiny bright face again. In addition the sun made a deal with the wind to blow the black clouds away, but it took some time and they had to work very carefully lest the clouds discover the plan and overthrow it. So we had to be patient until the plan went into effect. There was no doubt about it that the sun had plenty of energy and warmth to chase away the nasty black clouds and disperse them; we just had to wait for the fine hour. She just told it to alleviate the dark mood the dark shades caused, but I pointed it out to her, once we were alone, that it could be interpreted allegorically as well. She laughed; she had never thought about that.

Christmas was getting close. Would anybody celebrate it in these dark hours? Hardly. For once there were no trees available and neither candy nor other goodies, let alone toys for the children. But above all what was missing was love. And Christmas has always been the holiday of love. We were racking our brains: What could we do for the children? Something special, but since nothing was to be had and we couldn't even get extra food items, we just had to let it go. One lady who worked in the kitchen was very clever with folding paper to create birds, dogs, rabbits. It was only from newspaper, but it was something. She worked on them slowly, so every child would get one.

Mr. Gabor also showed up. He must have had a soft spot for children as he asked if it was all right for him to bring something for them that he would make himself.

"What do you have in mind?" we asked.

"Well, it isn't much," he admitted with a shy smile. "Just that I learned to whittle wood from my grandfather and I can make little dolls or animals for them. Do you think they would like them?"

"Would they ever. These little ones hardly have a toy. They would be delighted. Could you really do that for them?"

"I most certainly will. I just can't see the little tykes without anything for Christmas. It's cruel. It is enough how they are deprived of a normal life, at least they should have something of their own."

We were absolutely touched by his gesture.

IX.

One evening as I was about to fall asleep, I thought I heard a very faint humming of a long-not-heard tune. I must have been already half-asleep; otherwise I should have realized that it came from Zsuzsa. It was pleasant to listen to. It was the "Skaters' Waltz" from *Waldteufel*. I wondered why she was doing this. I didn't want to ask, but I must have stirred and she stopped.

"Don't stop, I like it."

She must have been a trifle nonplussed. "I'm sorry. I didn't mean to disturb you. I did not realize that an actual sound came out."

"What's wrong with that?" I interjected. "I told you I loved it. Were you already asleep perhaps and it was part of your dream?"

"If you must know, I was dreaming, but I was not asleep."

"What do you mean?" I asked, sitting up.

"All right, I'll let you in on my secret. As we are more or less locked in here and life outside is so terrible, I always return, before falling asleep, to happier times in my life. I am fooling myself; I know where I am, I know exactly what is going on and what might have happened to me and my family if I hadn't met you. But these escapades of mine help me to cheer up the forced existence here. So I pick another scene every night, usually from my childhood. Tonight, for example, I walked down under the barren tree-rows on Andrássy Street all the way to Heroes' Square. It is amazing how much detail I could conjure up. The *Opera House,* the renaissance-style buildings flanking the long avenue on both sides. I also 'noticed' the famous Lukács Pastry Shop. Have you ever been there?"

"Of course, what a question. I think everybody goes there at least once. It makes my mouth water just to think of it."

"Well," she continued, "I think I can tell you all the details of the kings' statues standing in the semicircle on Heroes' Square, as well as the tall column with its winged top standing in the middle. I never realized that I paid that much attention to it, but I must have been, otherwise I could not recall it all that vividly. So, after having crossed this huge square in my mind, I left behind those two beautiful buildings that look like Greek temples, you know, the Art Museum on the left and the Exhibition Hall on the right. As I neared the City Park, I began to hear the sound of faint music coming from the loudspeaker by the frozen lake, where I was headed. That's perhaps when I started to hum along and you heard me. A loud dream that even another can partake in. Have you ever heard the like?" and she laughed, chuckling like a gurgling brook.

It was contagious and I began to laugh too. I loved her for it. I didn't remember when I had laughed last, but the very idea was most amusing. Then she went on.

"It was a dry and sunny winter day for my dream excursion and I clearly heard the "Skaters' Waltz." I am very fond of it. I also love to skate and always hurried up with my school work to get out there soon and have more time to spend on the ice."

She stopped a second, then continued. "Now you know where I spent my evening today. And I don't know yet where my fancy will take me tomorrow night." She laughed again, this time a little self-consciously and asked if I thought her to be foolish.

"On the contrary. I like your escapade so much that I am going to be a copycat and take my own trips from now on. I'm sure it'll help. But Zsuzsa, if you can sing that well, why don't you teach the children to sing? You must know the words to some songs."

She looked at me. "Yes, I think I will. It'll be good for them."

I wanted so much to get some kind of present for Christmas for Oskar, for Zsuzsa. It was impossible. No normal activities could be carried out in these monstrous times. It was really more important that the children get something from Mr. Gabor. We were hoping that he could deliver those toys he had promised. The fighting was getting so intense that very few civilians risked going out. Only in extreme circumstances would anyone venture outside. Of course Mr. Gabor was a policeman; his duty kept him outside a lot.

It was sometime during the day when I accosted Zsuzsa. "Do you realize that we had no heavy bombing for quite some time now?"

That minute the sirens sounded to signal the oncoming air raid.

"Speak of the devil," laughed Zsuzsa, as we were descending the steps together with the children and the few adults who shared this abode now.

This shelter was an ordinary cellar that they used for keeping wood and coal in for heating. The wooden rails and thin walls dividing each tenant's own place were simply knocked out, thereby creating a large enough place for all who needed it and furnished it with a few benches, chairs, and a long table. There was room left on the floor to put the children down on blankets if they wanted to sleep. We got so used to these daily and nightly excursions to the shelter that it became a mere routine. One cannot be constantly afraid; it just seemed a nuisance. I think we all became a little fatalistic about it, whether we admitted it or not.

A woman overheard our conversation about the Allies not bombing us, as we continued this discussion once seated down there. She interrupted us: "Of course the Anglo-Saxons aren't coming anymore. The Russians are practically here. They are not going to bomb their allies. All we have to survive now is the Arrowcross's murders, the SS, and the Russian air raids and their artillery fire. Can you think of any more disaster befalling us?"

Tragic as it was, depicting the truth, we all laughed. It sounded so absurd if not outright comical.

Zsuzsa was very considerate and never brought up questions that might lead to my loss. Still she could not help evidently trying to find out something about me that might have puzzled her for some time.

"Don't you have any relatives in Budapest? I know nobody goes out now, but surely before the siege started I never heard you say that you saw this or that aunt, uncle, cousin, or what have you."

I had to smile. She was absolutely right.

"Well, Zsuzsa, my whole family on both sides is in Czechoslovakia, that part that used to belong to Hungary proper during the Austro-Hungarian Empire. My parents lived there too, they only moved to Budapest shortly before my birth. Maman's parents also moved here, but they passed away not such a long time ago. That's why."

"I hope you don't mind that I asked you."

"Not at all, I find it most natural. We have been together now for a while, you know quite a bit about me. I am very sorry that I cannot show you my home anymore. You would have enjoyed it; I also think you might have liked my parents too. I know they would have liked your company."

"Thank you, Agi. That is generous. All I can say is that I hope we can keep in touch and stay friends after this is all over."

"No doubt about this, Zsuzsa."

"By the way, do you plan on moving to Sweden after your marriage, or what?"

"Nothing has been decided yet. Oskar wants to take me to his mother as soon as possible, but no plans were worked out in detail yet."

One day Zsuzsa delighted the children with another story. But this story had a twist. The children had to guess part of it and this created a sensation among the little older ones.

"Once upon a time there was a prince who lost the maiden he loved. A magician put that maiden under a special spell that allowed her to be herself during the night, but she vanished every dawn. She was turned into a beautiful rose among a sea of roses in a special garden. Now this prince was heartbroken as he wanted to marry the lovely maiden. He was finally given a chance. If he recognized the rose into which his lovely bride had turned into, that would remove the spell. The prince was terribly worried. How could he recognize her among so many roses. There were pink and yellow roses, crimson colored and snow whites and every shade in between. Larger and smaller roses. He kept walking among the beds and looked carefully early morning. He was expecting a nod from the rose, a smile, as if roses could smile. He had no clue. He looked so sad and felt so forlorn, but he kept on looking and after he walked all over the garden, he started again. Then, all of a sudden he stopped and saw the rose. He knew then that he had found her. That instant the curse was removed as it had been promised and the rose turned back into the lovely maiden. Everybody in the kingdom rejoiced; they got married and lived happily ever after."

That was the end of the story. And then came the question: how did the prince recognize the rose. The children were baffled. Some asked for the clue, others wanted to gain some time and think about it. Among the latter group was Rozsika. Zsuzsa gave them till next day. The next morning after our dismal breakfast, Zsuzsa asked if they had thought about it. They all nodded.

"Any answer?"

"Nooo," they said sadly. Rozsika raised her hand. Everybody looked at her and she spoke. "I think I found out how."

Her eyes were shining as she spoke: "There must have been dew on every single rose, as you'd find it early morning. There was only one rose without the dew. That must have been the maiden, who was not there during the night to gather the dew as she was in her human form."

Zsuzsa applauded and the children followed.

"You are right Rozsika, absolutely right."

We saw Rozsika flushed for happiness.

"But how did you know?"

"My mother used to read a lot to me and I knew about the dew. I always wanted to see it but we never had a yard and I was never out so early, I just imagined what it must be like, perhaps like tiny raindrops after a shower, and if that maiden just turned into a rose when dawn came, she had no time to get it, so she must have been dry."

I thought that her mother was not exaggerating when she said that Rozsika was bright, and I could see in her the mother's traits that must have attracted Mr. Riley. Her eyes also shone when she just talked about her happier times. The poor soul. I made a mental note to let Mr. Riley know how special Rozsika was. I also turned to Zsuzsa: "That story is fantastic, how in the world did you make that up?"

"But I didn't. Someone asked me the same thing after having told me the story. I never guessed and I was a few years older than Rozsika is now. And whoever I told it to later on, nobody ever guessed it, except Rozsika. Quite a remarkable intellect she must harbor behind her somewhat sad blue eyes."

Christmas was upon us. Mr. Gabor came, true to his word, with two sacks and placed them under our beds.

"I would have liked to spend Christmas with you here, but I am afraid I was called on duty. My family is in the country, as I told you before, so I'll be thinking of them and you and let's hope for a real Christmas next year. I will look you up when I can again."

When the children were all in bed, we looked at some of the little toys. They were true to life, only the color was missing. He didn't forget any detail and not two of them were alike, although there were several horses, donkeys, chicken, goats and what have you. All very artistic.

We put one of these wooden animals and one folded paper form next to each child's plate and we sang Christmas songs. It seemed to us that these children were happier with that present than children who lived in happier circumstances and who got a lot of toys and fine food in addition. It was heartbreaking how surprised they were that they got anything at all and how they played with the toys, talked to them, named them, and clutched them. They even took them along when going to bed.

The children knew Zsuzsa's ability to tell stories and they came up next day with the request to use these animals in her next stories, I had no doubt that Zsuzsa would come up with many more delightful ones.

I hadn't heard from Oskar for a while, as there were no telephone lines working in our district. He came in the car on Christmas Day. I didn't sob this time, but I was on the verge and fought as hard as I could and luckily succeeded in behaving normally. Every time I laid my eyes on him, I saw my parents together with us. His presence was for me eternally linked to my father and mother.

"I wanted to bring you food, Agi, I know that that's what we need most. But I couldn't. There is none available. However, I still managed not to come empty-handed," and he pulled a small package from his pocket. He smiled. "Cheer up, we'll make it."

He kissed me and I proceeded to unwrap it.

"Actually," he said, "my mother sent it to me by a courier for you. She has no idea of our deprivations. I never mention it in my letters."

"I can understand that. I wouldn't either," I said. There, I pulled out the precious thing. It was a small golden brooch in the form of a bow with a tiny diamond in the middle. It was dainty and reflected the best and most refined taste. I hugged Oskar and thanked him.

"I guess I'll hang it on my chain next to the ring for the time being. Could I write a thank-you letter to your mother?"

"I'm sure she'd love that, not the 'thank you' I mean, but your letter. But considering the circumstances I think I'll do it and you'll make up for it after the war is over.

"I don't have a thing for you other than my love. I'm sorry."

"That's all I want. We can make up for it next Christmas for sure."

Then I told him about Rozsika. He smiled and said:

"We'll have to take care of her as soon as possible. Lucky for her that she has the unknown father in America. Does she know that she has lost her mother?"

I just shook my head. "I want to be able to give her not just hope but the result of steps taken to emigrate, before I inform her of her great loss. This way it'll be if not easy, but easier."

"You're a good psychologist. I can see you'll have no problem raising our children the right way, just as you were raised."

I kissed him and we felt very strongly that we belonged together. He left soon and promised to come whenever possible. I, in turn, begged him to stay indoors. He'd done enough already. He grinned, and off he went.

One would think that the fighting would have ceased at least for Christmas. But as we heard, the Arrowcross exhorted the people to go on and fight regardless of Christmas. So, though the noise lessened, it did not fade away and the next day the battle went on full force. Fires all over the city were getting more and more numerous. If you did not see them, you smelled it all. The smoke penetrated even the stones. The overcast sky kept these acrid smells low; they could not escape into the atmosphere. The cacophony was deafening, but we were so used to it by then, we barely paid attention to it. It became part of life. Or did life become part of death? For many, definitely. And one never knew which bomb or hand grenade had one's name on it.

But being with children and being young ourselves helped. We didn't really believe that we'd die. It was far away, no matter how realistically we saw and knew what was going on around us.

When I peeked out the window next morning, I saw huge, fluffy snowflakes coming down thickly, covering the street, the houses, everything. If you disregarded the din of the battle, it looked almost peaceful and was very soothing. Rozsika came in and stood silently by me, looking out.

"Oh, how lovely it would be to be outdoors and sit on a sled rushing down a slope. I really never had one, but my mother promised to get me one next winter. Do you think I'll get it some day?" and she looked up at me.

"Absolutely, we just have to wait to the end of the war and then life will be easier. You'll see."

She smiled faintly and with that hope she returned to play with the other children.

We woke up one day and had no water coming from the faucets. If it froze or broke, or if there was some other reason, we did not know.

So in addition to the usual hardships we had to face this new blow. We had to take turns going to the courtyard of that house and picking up snow in buckets, melting it for washing, cooking, even for drinking. We simply boiled it over the wood fire we had to build daily in an old stove. If it hadn't snowed I could't even imagine what we would have done. How could one live without water? Funny, who ever thought of its importance in normal times? I think we all took a lot of things for granted in peacetime. But now in these wretched conditions the value system changed. No gold and no money was precious; food, water, wood for heating, those were the vital matters to sustain life.

Our days got shortened too, as electricity failed and we had not too much kerosene left to burn in the little lamps. We had to be very careful, not knowing how long the siege would last.

About a week had passed in hard work and miserable conditions. Even the children became listless. No matter how hungry they were, they started to eat their food very slowly, almost showing signs of gagging on it. It was tasteless, monotonous, always the same. One of the children at the table complained to her neighbor: "If this is over, I shall never look at beans, lentils and dry peas as long as I live."

No one commented. We all understood. We could not blame her for her rebellion, and we were far from rebuking her by telling her that she should be happy she had food at all. She was too young to understand that many others had it worse. For her this was the worst and it was bad enough without the slightest exaggeration. Vying with each other about who had had it worse in this war was hopeless. Misery, destitution, degradation—all developed new and bottomless depths.

Oskar came over again. I was happy to see him but I was also outraged in my quiet ways that he ventured out. It was really taking his life in his hands. He wanted to talk to me in private, so we sat down in the small room I shared with Zsuzsa, who withdrew and kept busy with the children.

"Agi, I have to tell you about my immediate plans. As I already mentioned, we should leave here as soon as it is possible and go straight to my mother's. We'll get married there and then decide where to live. Is that agreeable to you?"

"Of course, darling. I can hardly wait, but I cannot forget Rozsika. I promised to take care of her."

"I thought of that and I think we should somehow take her along with us. I am sure it would be much easier for her to emigrate from Sweden. I mean, taking care of the formalities and correspondence would be faster there. It'd take some time here before things would go normally again. But before we do all that, I have a small trip ahead of me. Wallenberg has a plan that he wants to work out with the occupying Russian forces and the new Hungarian government residing now in *Debrecen*. We plan to go there as soon as it is feasible. It shouldn't take more than a day or two and we would return. He wants to establish a relief organization to feed, clothe, house, and in general take care of all those who survive this dreadful time and who need help. He worked out a list in which he briefly describes the awful things that took place here and to at least help physically those who had been wronged in such a way."

I was not exactly pleased with this plan and feared that it might take longer than a few days, although I knew that the city of *Debrecen* was not that far from Budapest by car.

"Couldn't I go along perhaps?" I suggested.

"I don't see any need for that, my darling. You could surely wait a few more days longer and also keep an eye on poor Rozsika. I promise to come back as soon as possible. Then we start our own life. We get married in Sweden and have our honeymoon, then I plunge into work. Is this all acceptable?"

I kissed him and nodded. What else could I do? Tell him that I feel very lonely and abandoned? In view of all those homeless and tortured, not to mention killed souls? How could I show such selfishness? He brought up another subject: money.

"I am leaving money with you. Not just *pengös*, but Swedish *Kroner*. I have enclosed an official paper proving that I, a Swedish citizen, have given to you so much, since you are my fiancee. I am leaving on a trip and have no intention of carrying that much cash with me. Neither can I leave it safely at the Embassy, as most everyone has already left and there is no knowing who will go there and what they'd do. Hide it if possible on your person, safe in underwear or something. Perhaps you can sew a money bag or two. These are times when such precautions are a must. Yes, make it sure you have the paper explaining the foreign currency's origin together with it. Should it ever be necessary to explain how you got it, that should do."

"I'll do it, but I tell you I won't have a minute's peace until you return to me from *Debrecen*. Don't forget, all I have in this life now is you."

His face and eyes turned very sober and his self-assurance faded away. He stood there a split-second like a forlorn child, as if just realizing that I had lost my parents and had none other than him. Maybe he felt a twinge of remorse. He looked at me, his face turning sad, then he smiled faintly, hugged me, and kissed me. "Agi, you are my life, I won't stay away longer than necessary."

I merely murmured a faint-hearted "Thank you, Oskar."

He left and I put the money in the drawer to take care of its proper hiding place later on, once the children were in bed.

X.

Very fierce fighting broke out. No civilians were outside. Shots from long and close range alternated with a rain of incendiary bombs thrown down from airplanes. We were in the middle of a battlefield, locked in the houses, waiting for the storm to blow over.

I hadn't seen Oskar since his last visit and there was no way to find out just when he would leave. Not even Mr. Gabor had shown up. He might have been positioned in some other part of the city, of course.

We kept telling each other that the darkest hours had arrived, so the expected dawn inevitably following the blackness could not be far. But in such circumstances time has the quality of creeping. You feel the weight of not every minute but every second. Death hovering above us constantly, the hunger pains, the lack of facility to keep us sufficiently clean, the crowded quarters, the helpless children, the uncertainty of what to expect from the new occupying forces—all that weighed on our consciousness.

I am not sure if my opinion is valid, but I couldn't help thinking that if we had been there under the same conditions, but without the children, only adults, we would have complained much more and we would have gotten on each other's nerves. But, with the presence of the children, our obligation to help them make their miserable life more tolerable, to try to sustain hope in them, we all disciplined ourselves and did our most and best. We all knew that as adults we had already developed some sort of thicker skin and that those children were going to be marred for life by this existence, and if we handled them with love and patience, we could soften the raw edges and cruel jolts of fate for them.

One morning, it was barely dawn yet, Zsuzsa sat up in bed and asked me, "Do you hear it?"

I sat up too, and listened, I heard nothing. I got out of bed and approached the window to peek out at the edge of the wooden shutters. I still heard nothing and swiftly crawled back to bed, under the cover to keep from freezing.

"What am I supposed to hear, Zsuzsa?"

She smiled. "The silence!"

"Silence?" I muttered. "Whatever do you mean?"

"The shooting stopped! Don't you realize, it must be over!"

I sat nonplussed. Could it be? "Let's just wait," I said cautiously.

In a little while we heard strange voices, men talking in an alien tongue; we did not understand a word. Though we did not know Russian, we had heard it over the radio before and this did not sound like it. We peeked out again from behind the shutters and saw Rumanian soldiers. So that's what we heard. We found out later, that the Russians sent ahead Rumanian forces who were fighting within the Red Army, to see how much resistance there still was. Once they found out that the city was helpless, the military must have withdrawn and only civilians were around.

Then the Russian soldiers appeared. No one dared go out, not knowing what the *Russkies* would do. We all remembered from history how after every victorious battle the generals let their soldiers plunder, loot, and rape. It was the victors' reward. It had been written about the armies of Alexander the Great, Julius Caesar, the Cruisaders in the Middle Ages, Napoleon's army, and so on. It was the Red Army's turn now. And we were the defeated enemy.

A few civilians appeared slowly on the street besides the soldiers, as we watched from the window. Most of them pulled sleds on which we spotted covered bodies, or uncovered ones. It was still bitter cold and intermittent snow showers covered the grim sights with a fresh white blanket.

I felt like going to the Embassy to find out if Oskar had left yet, though I was pretty sure he had, or he would have come. The sooner he left, the sooner he would be back, I consoled myself. Now that the fighting was over, I felt a surging impatience welling up in me. I wanted to have all this misery behind me and start a new life instantly. It was enough.

Having been locked in for so long, we just had to go out and walk on the street, if only a few blocks' distance. We kept the children in for the time being, of course, as everything was shrouded in uncertainty. It was only during daylight that we could go out. There was still a curfew for civilians after dark, and the days were still short toward the end of January.

On clear days the sun often blushed in a blood shade upon witnessing the horrors down below. The nearby clouds reflected that shame in turning crimson and slowly blotting out the view, forming a thick, woolen-like blanket for a screen. Further up north, where the demons of hatred carried out hitherto unimaginable crimes on a colossal scale, the sun paled into a barely visible shine in the leaden sky. I heard later on from a camp survivor who revisited the sites that he saw no birds there. An eerie silence greeted him, heavy with the ghosts of the past. The only sound he heard was the wind whistling a mournful dirge.

We arranged with the few adults that they watch the children for half an hour, while we'd go down with Zsuzsa. We didn't have to go long in the direction of the Great Boulevard. We were both stunned at the sights. Bodies were lying all over, civilians and soldiers, little children, parts of bodies, an arm here, half a torso there. One side street had a tumbril-like contraption made of wood. It looked like the ones described in books about the French Revolution, in which they took the victims to the guillotine. This tumbril here was not very different, except it contained a few bodies thrown onto it, not before they were guillotined, but after death had already claimed them. The power lines were hanging loosely, often torn from the poles lining the streets. There were neither streetcars nor buses around, only sporadic foot traffic. At the middle of the boulevard where *Rákóczi* Street crossed it, stood a Russian barishnya, a policewoman directing the so-called traffic with a yellow and red triangle-shaped little flag in each hand. We noticed that she had slanted eyes. Mongol? Tatar? Other people carried bundles; some pulled sleds. Bodies of people and children of all ages were piled on them.

Many buildings were in total ruins, others stood partially intact. Broken bricks, stone in tall heaps, alternated with damaged but still existing houses. One department store, the *Corvin,* or rather what was left of it, was unrecognizable. Only its outer four walls stood, some four stories high. The inside seemed to have burned down completely and the windows dotting each floor across the whole façade, including the entrance, were blackened holes staring like unseeing blind eyes. We stared back, shocked. As we went by we noticed that people entered this place with their bundles and deposited them there. Soon it was packed with bodies. Who decided such a thing or did everyone had the same idea? Only the extreme cold weather and the anesthetizing snow saved us from the outbreak of typhoid.

Suddenly a shot went by above our heads, whistling in high C with a slight slurring accompaniment. We ducked, so did others. "What was that?" There were more shots little farther away. Who was shooting? We thought it was over and so did evidently all those out on the street. Well, you heard immediately that the shots were coming from Buda, or directed against Buda, still in German hands. And we also learned that all the bridges had been mined and detonated when the Germans fled Pest, and after they crossed them to reach Buda where they continued their fighting.

We decided to return to the Home fast because of those shots. We glanced around. It had started to snow again and as it came down softly, blurring the sights into an almost impressionistic image, it also lent the picture an incredible, unreal quality. Quite unexpectedly Zsuzsa poked me and grimaced, rolling her eyes sideways.

"What's the matter?" I asked, worried that something had befallen her.

"We're being followed," she whispered barely audibly through her teeth.

"What?" I gasped. "By whom?" and I shot a side glance. My heart started pumping. There were two Russian soldiers at our heels. "What do they want from us?" I whispered to Zsuzsa.

"Guess," was her only answer.

We automatically hastened our steps and made it to the entrance of the Home, still flying the White-Cross flag. We rushed up the stairs, our followers pursuing us without saying one word. They carried rifles with bayonets at the end. Their uniform was a dirty beige, of a material that reminded one of a coarse horse-blanket. Their *épaulettes* were red and the coats were very long, needed in their cold homeland. We closed the door behind us once we reached the first floor, which we occupied with the children. No sooner had the children ran to us and hugged us— were they perhaps afraid that we would abandon them too?—the two soldiers banged on the door with their rifle butts and just about broke it down, when one of the women opened it. We all stood frozen, and they in turn seemed to be almost taken aback by seeing that many children crowding the place. The little ones clung to us, gaping at the soldiers, some afraid, some full of curiosity. I don't know just what must have gone through the mind of a little boy, who stepped forward and held his hand out as if wanting something. Did he think they were there to give him candy? No one uttered a sound and the two Russians were perhaps the only ones who understood the child and the situation. They said something, we didn't know what, and left. We heaved a sigh. Well, not for too long. It was not more than an hour before the same rifle-banging was heard again.

"What now?" we looked at each other. Did they bring more soldiers with them? We had to open the door. Only the same two returned and they had two bags, paper bags, in their hands. The children ran up to them. Somehow they knew. Sugar cubes were in the bags and they gave them to the children, who shrieked with delight. The two of them just smiled and left.

Not many people believed this scene when we told them about it later on. They certainly had different experiences and stories to tell, especially young girls, but older women weren't exempt either, depending on the drunken state of the soldiers.

I had a slight injury on my big toe that would not heal and because of it I had difficulty putting on my shoes. So finally I decided to go to the hospital to seek help. I had to wear a man's shoe on my right foot, otherwise I would have had to go barefoot, and it was still cold. My own shoe would not go over it without causing strong pain. As I was limping along in the two different shoes, a Russian soldier took my arm and started talking. I didn't know what he was talking about, but I knew exactly what he wanted. I also knew that if I shouted for help nobody would come to my aid. He was the conqueror, we were the defeated enemy. I racked my brain about how to get out of this predicament and slowly I realized that there was no way out. Now, I didn't know any Russian, but we had all picked up a few words here and there, so suddenly I understood a question he put to me: "Kuda idjos?" (Where are you going?)

"To the hospital," I said in broken Russian.

He understood. His grip loosened and after a few steps he turned away from me and left. I could hardly believe this. I was so relieved, I could have waltzed to the hospital in spite of hurting toe and clumsy shoes.

At first I couldn't figure out what had really happened. Then, as I slowly continued on my way, I put two and two together. Hearing that I was headed to the hospital, he concluded that I was sick. Maybe he convinced himself that I had V.D. So he got cold feet and fled. When this occurred to me, I could hardly keep from laughing. I was the last person on earth who could make up such a story. I am typically the person with the so-called *l'esprit d'escalier*. That is, I can never come up with the right answer, let alone a perfect squelch. I could think of it only long after I should have said it. In this case, this was perhaps the only deterrent that made him leave me alone. Nothing else would have stopped him. It happened to be true that I was going to the hospital, and that saved me. That he concluded for the wrong reason, was his mistake and my luck.

It was absolutely amazing how news traveled on invisible wings and with the speed of light. You heard of atrocities now committed by the Russians. They would take anyone at random to *malinki robot*. That means little work. In reality it could be anything. Raping women, taking men for work in the fields, or packing them up on trucks and taking them to any length of distance. Some of them never returned and no one knew of their fate. All this was, however, sporadic, not a systematic organized arrangement and it only took place during the first weeks of their arrival.

One morning a woman came bringing a letter to Zsuzsa. It was from her parents. The mother was fine at that Home where the Arrowcross did not return after it turned out that the children were Catholics, even if non-Aryan, although the Arrowcross were not informed of this. Zsuzsa's father ended up in that Home too, in the middle of the worst fighting. The Arrowcross would not give peace and ransacked what they could and killed with boundless gusto. They took the children from the Home he had been working in. He barely escaped and ran to his wife. The children vanished without a trace, but he managed to stay in this other Home under the care of his wife. He developed dysentery, which was widespread all over. Zsuzsa's brother was not heard from yet.

For the time being we all stayed put. I, for one, had no place to go to. Zsuzsa decided one day to go and see if their old home was damaged or if they couldn't return there perchance. She told me that it had been allotted to a *Horthy* officer and his family. Zsuzsa recalled how her father had admonished them to take good care of the furniture and everything in it, until he returned. The current tenants were just staring at him as if he had been a lunatic. They certainly never expected either him or his family to return. They knew that the Jews were taken to be extirpated, to use the very word of an extreme right-wing cabinet member who fully cooperated with the Nazis, and was sure of their victory. The family felt the same way and they took it for granted that everything there would belong to them. They just about paled when they opened the door and Zsuzsa appeared. She told me that they were polite out of fear that the surviving family would want to get rid of them. Well, no family had that kind of power, but the authorities, as soon as some kind of order started to form, deprived all those who had obtained anything through the extreme right-wing parties. So, Zsuzsa and her family got back their old place almost intact. One room, she said, had been damaged by a bomb; they could not enter it until it was rebuilt. They happened to cram extra furniture, into that room to make room for this new family's belongings; they also put in there clothes, dishes and what have you. Unless that family took anything before the bombing took place, it should be there and that certainly would come in very handy as anyone could see that it would take a very long time before anything was going to be available in that wartorn city and country.

Now that the fighting was over, at least in Pest, everyone was anxious to start their new life, built on the old ruins or anew. Young and healthy people started to go to the country to get food. That was first and foremost on everybody's mind in the hungry city. Zsuzsa knew some people living in the country; so did I. But we had the children to take care of. Still, getting food was so paramount that after a swift consultation we decided to gather some clothes and go off to barter. Rozsika wanted to come with me so badly I almost had no heart to talk her out of it, but I had to. We were to walk quite a distance and in deep snow.

We took off one morning in February as soon as daylight broke and walked to the city limits following the streetcar lines. The cemeteries are located there at the end of *Kerepesi* street. As we walked by, a horrible sight was revealed in front of us through the open gates: endless rows of mountains bodies heaped on top of each other, a few rows crosswise, and on top of it another row laid down the opposite way. It was unreal, like a nightmare come true. I remembered how my dear father used to relate some of his experiences from the First World War when they buried the fallen comrades in a similar fashion in a large ditch, pouring lime over them.

We trudged across seemingly boundless snow-covered fields. A few black crows cawed raw, expressing their indignation of not finding any food. We just about understood them and shared their feelings. One small town that was not very far from Pest was half-demolished. There we spotted the sign of a drugstore, its door ajar, some bottles left in the greatest disarray. In no time some pedestrians there asked us if we came from Pest, if the fighting was over, what the situation was. They in turn told us that the Russian soldiers broke into the drugstore and to the horror of the onlookers they drank the alcohol that was for burning, used in lamps. It was totally undistilled and terrible. To the people's amazement none of them seemed to get sick from it. They must have been used to such strong spirits. Then we saw another sight. A dead horse was lying on the street, and several women were fighting over its carcass to carve some meat from it. Both Zsuzsa and I turned away in horror. But Zsuzsa was the stronger between the two of us and by a long shot the less finicky.

When we finally reached the home where Zsuzsa's friends lived, we were offered supper. By that time it was late afternoon and we were quite tired. It wasn't just that we had walked a good many kilometers and were in a weak condition due to poor nourishment for quite some time, but the snow made every step hard. I could hardly wait to get to bed. Still the idea of a dinner around a table in a clean room among friendly people was very alluring; but what followed made me dreadfully ashamed. I shall never forget my embarrassment as long as I live. They announced with great pride that we would get a great delicacy, horse liver, fried with onions. My heart sank. I had never liked liver of any kind. For some reason it made me gag and I refused to eat it. It wasn't that it was the liver of a horse, but the liver itself. There was some boiled parsnip too, that was all I ate. No one criticized me, but I could imagine what they said about the pampered young lady from Budapest who refused to eat horse when supposedly they were starving.

Zsuzsa ate her fill and we slept under the eiderdown like two babies. We continued our trip the next morning and reached *Juliska's* place some hours later. She used to work for my father and I had already been in that house, at the house-warming party arranged by my father. He always took great pride in helping all his employees to reach as high a standard of living as was feasible and he often arranged all kind of help in promoting it. This house was built of stone and had three rooms, a kitchen, and a nice entry. There was no toilet inside; the husband, who came from a peasant family, refused such a "filthy" place incorporated in his house. So they had an outhouse and used chamberpots during the night.

Juliska was very friendly. She was shocked when she heard of my parents' fate. I saw that she had difficulty holding back her tears. I was thankful that she did, or else I would have broken down completely. The less said, the better, especially with semi-strangers. I explained why we came and she assured me that she had flour, cornflour, and oil to cook with. First she refused to take anything for it, but when she noticed a pair of lovely shoes, her eyes gave her away and she accepted it and a blouse that took her fancy.

Such items had tremendous value as most people had lost a great deal; others had nothing left. As our money began to lose its value, no one wanted it. Hence started the bartering and it lasted a long time.

By way of redeeming my shattered ego, I did eat horsemeat at Juliska's. It was ground and made into a meatloaf that was really tasty. She used a lot of pepper and that suppressed its somewhat sweetish taste.

On the way back we noticed a Russian officer who had his son with him, a tiny replica of his father, at most eight years old, in authentic Russian uniform. It almost looked like a stage scene from an operetta. Alas, it had a grim reality behind it. Did he bring the son all the way from Russia? Was their home destroyed, was there no mother or anyone else to leave the child with? I shall never find out.

It wasn't the only thing I shall never know. When we got back, everyone rejoiced. Not only at our safe return but because of the great loot we carried. It was almost life-saving. It was a marvel what they could cook from it. Zsuzsa and myself were exhausted, but happy to be back and having been of help to the many hungry mouths.

Miraculously the telephone was restored and so was electricity. This was a great help. I called the Embassy immediately, but nobody knew anything of Oskar or of his whereabouts. I asked for Per Anger, his old colleague, but I was informed that he had left some time ago and would not return. Mr. Danielsson had also returned to Sweden. So I tried the Swiss Embassy, but Mr. Lutz had left for good.

What I was trying to find out, besides the time when Oskar had left, was to start Rozsika's emigration. I wanted to get in touch with Mr. Riley through a telegram or letter to let him know that Rozsika had survived the Holocaust and the siege of Budapest, but that the mother did not. But evidently it was too early and everybody said one had to wait a while before such steps could be taken.

Slowly the bodies disappeared from the streets. The rubble was cleared away even if the houses that collapsed stayed intact with their dead buried underneath them for a long time to come. The farmers started to come to the capital from the nearby villages. They loaded their horse-drawn carriages with all kinds of food; in turn they took home clothing, furniture, often jewelry, watches. Apropos watches: That was something odd. The Russian soldiers were crazy about them. Some of them sported six or seven on their arms and proudly showed them off. They couldn't get enough. Didn't they have any at home, we wondered. Then we remembered having seen posters with Zsuzsa that had appeared earlier, perhaps late summer, or was it fall? It depicted an arm from which a hand wearing a watch was torn off, with blood dripping from it. The caption ran: 'This is what the Russian soldiers will do to you.' We never paid attention; it was sheer propaganda. I am sure they did not tear off hands, but they took watches where they could, that was a fact.

There were lots of homes and apartments that stood empty. Their former inhabitants had not come back yet or maybe never would. New people moved in, whose homes had been destroyed. They knew that if the original owner returned they'd have to leave or share the place.

Our problem was now what to do about the children. Most adults were anxious to return to their lives or start whatever existence they could. But we could not leave those poor darlings alone. What to do? First of all it would have been very desirable to find some larger, more adequate quarters. We went on the prowl with Zsuzsa. She knew some welfare-minded people who used to help orphans and in general took care of the needy and she suggested we go to a hospital not very far from us. It was also packed with people who slowly left the shelter and returned to their homes and families if they had any. But she met someone there who was very helpful and gave us another address where we could find people who could and no doubt would help with our problem.

It is amazing what difference there is among people. Some are born leaders and organizers no matter what the circumstances. Others just look out for their own personal needs. Then there are those who could never even look out for themselves, let alone help others. Well, we were lucky to meet a man who although he had barely survived and had lost everything he used to have, was ready—and in fact had already gathered people around himself—to establish a self-relief organization. He did not wait for any state or government help that might come later on. He knew that help was needed instantly and there he was to give it. He was not just offering help in vague terms, but he already had an existing house with enough furniture in it and some necessary supplies, like linen, bedding, food, dishes, pots and pans, etc. He wanted us to bring the children over in two days' time and if possible stay with them until enough help came to relieve us. He also thanked us for the wonderful work we had done in saving the children as well as caring for them in those dreadful times.

Zsuzsa's parents returned to their old home and Zsuzsa was very willing to come to the new Children's Home to help out as long as it was necessary. I naturally went; it was to be my new home until Oskar arranged our future. Two older women who had not yet found anyone returning from their families decided to stay and work. At least they also had a roof above their heads and food. They liked to care for the children.

This man who got us the large home also organized a small army of youngsters who were going to the country to get supplies. He had only a small office but he meticulously gathered all data of all the children and filed them. There were also lists made out, endless lists of children looking for their parents. They posted them in every official place to reach a wide circle of the population.

Later on when the American Joint Distribution Committee was established in Budapest he got in touch with them and managed to get a lot of help. He also started the emigration of those who wished to go overseas or some Western European countries. In time his office was attached to the Joint and greatly enlarged in duties that he either took care of himself or skillfully delegated to an ever-growing army of employees.

The young girl who swam out of the Danube had to be hospitalized as she developed some lung trouble. She had been suffering silently, but now that we were liberated from the Nazi yoke, she mentioned it and was advised to go into a hospital and seek help.

People came daily to ask for employment, many among them to take care of the children. Among those who came to apply for the jobs, I spotted a young girl, the daughter of an old teacher of mine, actually one of the best I ever had. She used to teach German language and literature. She was so imbued with the love of the subject, especially with Goethe, that she inspired us in a way no other teacher of mine ever did. I remember how her eyes had shone when she related to us incidents from Goethe's childhood or when she explained to us this or that ballad. Instead of feeling that it was a burden to memorize them, we vied with each other as to who knew them better. As she also liked singing, we sang all the verses that had been sat to music, like the *Heidenröslein*, etc. The hours we had with her seemed to pass in five minutes and I think all of us regretted when the bell rang, inidicating the end of the lesson.

Now, when Elli recognized me, she came to me to ask if we could use her. I happened to inquire about her parents. She stopped talking, looked at me, and did not talk. I had an awful foreboding feeling of what she was going to tell me. Before she could gather herself, I told her freely that I lost my parents in an airraid. She still said nothing; finally in a strained voice she said, "I'm terribly sorry, Agi, for that, but to me it sounds like a dignified, almost beautiful death," she paused a second, "if death can be beautiful."

I looked at her with horrified eyes and could not bring myself to ask whatever she meant. But she continued: "We were in the Ghetto. One day I went out to take care of something, they stayed home. When I returned, I saw the two of them with others from that house lying frozen in blood on the pavement in front of the house." Her voice trailed away, she had no tears, perhaps she had shed them all before. "I have nowhere to go. Perhaps I could help with children younger than I am, to do whatever is needed."

"Of course you may stay. I simply don't know what to say, Elli. I loved and respected your dear mother with many others. I will always remember her."

Then I thought of the irony of it. She breathed German culture and she instilled the love of it into all her students and it was the Germans who murdered her brutally together with her husband.

Before we left that crammed quarters that we occupied before and during the siege, I left a note, rather a letter for Oskar with the concierge. I also left one for Mr. Gabor. I put in it our new address and telephone number. I also left this new address at the old Embassy office where he stayed when in Pest. The original was in Buda, that one could not be approached yet. I also decided to write a letter to Oskar's mother. After all, I never said thank you for that lovely gift she had sent me. It looked to me like a family heirloom.

Oskar was right in telling me not to write personal letters through the Embassy courier, but now there was no more excuse in not saying thank you and writing a friendly letter. So I took care of that and went to the Main Post Office to send it together with my ardent wishes for our meeting. I also explained in that letter that Oskar had gone on a small trip to the country and once back, we would, he would arrange the necessary steps for us to go up North. I also added how I was looking forward to that meeting. Now that I had no more family of my own she was going to be my family, or Oskar's family was going to be mine too. I shed a few tears when I wrote that, but that was the way I felt. I was hoping she would understand.

It was the first time I went toward downtown, the oldest district in Pest. It was very heavily damaged. The whole row of elegant hotels by the Danube between the Elizabeth and Chain bridges were all razed to the ground. Many other buildings were fully hit, a high heap of rubble indicating where they used to stand.

The children got used to the new quarters fast. They were much larger and the sunny windows helped to cheer up everything. Only a few of them shared a room, and they could choose whom they wanted to have for rommates, That pleased them enormously. To make a decision! They had never had that privilege before. Then some of them started to ask when their parents would come for them. We tried to explain that we would have to wait quite a while as the war was still raging west of us and some of the parents were in Germany, or so we thought. Rozsika asked me why her mother did not come. I didn't want to lie anymore, so contrary to my original decision I had to talk to her and tell her that she passed away during the siege in the hospital. I also added that I promised her to take care of her myself. I also explained that a very close relation wanted to have her in America and as soon as it was feasible we would arrange the papers for her emigration.

I let her cry a while. Then as her sobs slowly decreased she started to talk to me: "I remember everything she ever told me. Why did she have to die?" And she started crying again. I wiped her tears from her hot cheeks.

"I will always remember and do what she said. I will," she reassured her promise to herself. Then she turned to me: "You know, Agi, I think she will watch me from up above, I feel it. She did not abandon me."

"I'm sure she will," I said with tears rolling down my cheeks.

She cried some more, the poor soul, and buried her golden curls in my lap. I held her tight and stroked those curls. They must have come from her father, as the mother had dark hair and eyes.

She was an inquisitive child and slowly she started to ask questions about America. She insisted that I had to go with her to America. No library was open yet for me to go to and brush up on the subject, so I told her as little as I knew.

I remembered that Rozsika's mother had told me that the little girl's father lived close to Seattle, in the Pacific Northwest. So I drew a rough map for her of Europe, the Atlantic, then the whole United States, and showed at the other edge where she was going to live.

"But aren't there Indians who scalp you?"

I couldn't help laughing. "Where in the world did you find out this information, Rozsika?"

"Mama read me a lot and I also read as much as I can. I love to find out new things, the more the better."

Amazing, I thought. It was in her blood and in her upbringing. That's double strength. The strongest bond.

Now all we had to do was to really start the steps to begin our new life. But where was Oskar? He must have left quite some time ago, if he hadn't he would have come to me and he did not come. I wasn't surprised that the trip took longer than the two days at most that he mentioned. It was also possible that he had to wait to see this General Malinovsky he was talking about, or, perhaps the negotiations took longer. Where was he anyway? And who else went along besides Raoul Wallenberg? I found the answer to that at the office, where I could not help going twice a week to see if they had heard anything.

I found out that they had had a chauffeur to drive the car, the very same faithful man who traveled with Wallenberg all over the country in the most adverse conditions. His name was Vilmos Langfelder, an engineer by profession. When I went there the next time, I spotted the green Studebaker, the car Wallenberg usually used. I knew it well as Oskar also used it when Wallenberg needed a larger car. My heart leaped, and I took the stairs by threes as I ran up to see him. He must just have gotten back. It was their car. No such luck. They informed me that they had taken another car this time that they found more suitable for this special trip. I also made the acquaintance of a Dr. László Pető, who happened to be there in the *Tátra utca* office when I stumbled in quite breathlessly. I didn't know who he was, but I presented my case and myself and said that I was Oskar's fiancée. He was most obliging and extremely polite. His charming manners put one completely at ease. Upon my inquiries he said the following:

"I was in the car with Oskar, Wallenberg, and Vilmos on our way to *Debrecen*. We were still at the outskirts of the city when our car collided with a Russian truck. There was a big commotion, though no injury or very little damage was done. The Russians swore and wanted to take Langfelder with them to arrest him for the slight dent he had caused. I don't even think he really did it, rather the other way around, but naturally we could not bring that up. The conquering soldier is always right. Well, to cut it short, there was already a motorcycle escort following us to take us safely to Malinovsky's headquarters in *Debrecen*. However, as we had to stop on account of the slight collision, we were talking and one of the Russians said that the fight was almost over in Pest and it would take only a few more days and Buda would also be liberated. When I heard that, I decided to stay behind, as my parents were in Buda and I wanted to see them and be with them, the sooner the better."

I just nodded, envying him that he had parents who survived in Buda.

"They understood my decision," he went on, "and I did not get back to the car with them. They proceeded without me. By the way, one of the Russian escort helped Langfelder not to get arrested, as he explained to them that this car enjoyed diplomatic immunity, so they left, As to where they are now, what they have accomplished I don't know yet. And we shall only find it out when they return, I'm anxiously awaiting that too, my dear lady. In the meantime I am sorry I did not stay, for as it looks it might take a while before Buda is going to be liberated. I heard that there are terribly bitter fights going on, worse than we had in Pest."

With that information he took his leave, expressing his wish to get together with us once things quieted down and life began to flow in its normal way again. Before he left, though, he asked me what I was doing and after having found out, he was very appreciative of what I told him briefly. He also gave me his temporary address and phone, and also his parents' permanent address.

After I left, I sadly realized that I wasn't much smarter, and I slowly retraced my steps toward the new Home.

As I was tossing and turning in my bed, thinking of all that *Dr. Pető* had told me, I kept wondering if Oskar would have reacted to the news the same way *Dr. Pető* did. Would he have stayed behind to meet me again in my parents' home, had I stayed there and if the bomb hadn't destroyed it? Or would he have gone ahead to take care of what he felt was his duty, and only afterwards return to see if we survived the siege? I shall never have the answer to this question. It was hypothetical; still it puzzled me. The very idea, however, that this problem occurred to me indicated clearly that I was disappointed in Oskar's behavior. I expected more protection. Didn't he agree so whole-heartedly to my poor parents' demand that I stay home with them, as the Russian Army was to march in and do who knows what? Well? The Red Army did make the move and come to think of it, only the presence of the children saved us with Zsuzsa from the frequently complained fate they doled out to the conquered women. I'm not saying that I did not admire Oskar's heroic, unselfish help to so many people. But charity, protection, care should start at home, or at least include one's loved ones too. Was I perchance already taken for granted by him? Or, on the other hand, had I become selfish and was I pitying myself unduly? I pondered over that a while and could not objectively decide. But I had that nagging feeling that I had been neglected, if not downright abandoned. I also kept wondering what my dear parents would think of the situation. I couldn't help feeling that they would have been on my side, even Papa, who was the personification of duty, honor, and integrity.

One day Vera came to see me.

"How did you find me?" I asked her, most astonished.

"I heard from several people where you spent the siege, I just couldn't come. I also heard the tragedy and wanted to tell you that both Mother and myself feel terrible and would like to help you with whatever we can."

"Thank you, Vera. I am managing slowly working with the children helped me survive, not forget, just endure. How are you doing these days? Any news from your father?"

"We got some cards for a while and nothing lately, but we still hope that he survived. How about Oskar? Where is he these days.?"

"Good question." And I told her what I knew. She made a face I wasn't sure how to interpret. "Why did you let him go?"

"Let him go?" I asked, astonished. "How could I have kept him back?"

"Just by telling him that you needed him and he shouldn't have left you all by yourself. It would have been his duty to stand by you."

"Yes Vera, and no."

"What do you mean 'no'?"

"Well, how should I explain? I am opposed to forcing somebody, anybody against his will. If he felt he had to go, let him go. Had he stayed here because I begged him, I would not just have felt guilty but his staying here would have had no value in my eyes. Only if he had chosen to stay on his own. Can you understand that?"

"I can," Vera answered, "but let me tell you, with this attitude you won't get anything in life. People get away with what they can. If you don't fight for what you want, you'll be in trouble. It's that simple. People are no angels!"

"Thanks for the tip, but I still feel that he should have stayed here by his own conviction, not by my asking him."

"Are you testing him?"

"I wouldn't phrase it that way. I just am, to be perfectly frank, disappointed."

"I can believe that. If it happened to me, I would be furious," she admitted.

"How is your friend Peter? Are you still going together?" I asked to change the subject.

"We spent a lot of time together, as he was hiding and I helped him with Mother's approval, but to tell you the truth, he is having such jealous fits that it frightens me and I decided to break the relationship." She stopped talking, perhaps to ponder over the slipped word "relationship," but then she went on: "Lately he started to call me his *Desdemona*. He threatened me several times that if I as much as looked at another man, he was going to kill me. I am really frightened."

"That's terrible, Vera. He must be insane. Did you tell your mother about it?"

"I didn't want to alarm her but I have to do something, I'm not sure who to turn to."

She made me promise to go and visit them soon and she left, rather abruptly. Maybe she regretted her indiscretion. After all, how could I help her? But I knew that she needed good advice and I could not come up with any.

Such unruly passions were totally alien to me. I only read of them in books and withdrew instinctively from such characters in life. I felt I did not belong with them. Maman once said something funny about both Father and me: according to her we were born with a *sordino*. The little bridge that mutes the sound on the violin was built into us to restrain loud, harsh sounds. Liking pastel colors and not overspiced food went along with that; also hearing the small voices and sound of silence was part of it. If you enjoy the bubbling of brooks, the humming of bees on a field of wild flowers on a hot summer day when nothing stirs, air and time stand still, then you are beyond the reach of the drummers and trumpets. They are outside of the frame within which you lived.

I racked my brain as to how to help Vera. I ought to come up with something. She needed help. I needed time.

One day an elderly withered-looking woman with very dark purplish shadows under her sunken eyes came in, looking for me by name. I looked at her; there was a vague familiarity about her, but for the life of me I could not place her. She looked at my searching eyes and said in a low voice: "You don't recognize me, I am Mrs. Révai."

"Of course, forgive me, please," I muttered, embarrassed.

"My dear, don't feel bad, it happens to all of us. I heard you need workers and I am a candidate." She stopped a second, sighed, and added: "For any kind. I need it," she added for emphasis.

That woman was the wife of a rather prominent citizen and exercised quite a bit of charity before the war and even during it. What could have happened to her, I wondered. If she read my mind or was about to explain, I don't know, but she started talking in a low, monotonous voice, a stark contrast to her old lively one. It sounded as if someone read an uninteresting speech without the slightest interest in its content.

"I lost my husband, I lost all three of my sons in the Ukraine. Marika, my only daughter caught some dreadful disease at the beginning of the siege and she passed away, leaving her child with some relations of her husband's who also died. I have no one left; I don't have a roof over my head; I wish I had died too. Alas, I'm alive, hungry, and most unhappy. Could you have pity on an old lady? Could you give me work, anything, and perhaps I could live in. I love children and can think of no other place to go to."

I stood frozen, listening to one more war story. Was there no end to them? Of course I found work for her, a tiny room and a kind word here and there.

When I went to bed that evening, I had a vague feeling that if I hadn't heard her story yet, there was something very familiar about it. I couldn't figure out what it was, but my dream brought it forth. Big waves followed each other, dirty water growing and mounting and swallowing everything, streets, carriages, animals, houses. I woke up in cold sweat. Not again! was I having a nightmare? I drank no dodanella. What was the matter with me? Was I losing my mind? Then it hit me. The short story we had read in school such a long time ago during the French lessons pushed itself to my consciousness and I saw the Garonne river as it left its bed. Zola described it so vividly in his L'Inondation that I visualized it and Mrs. Révai's story reminded me of it. Therein too, everyone dies, all the young ones, and the old grandfather survives and he witnesses as his daughters, in-laws, grandchildren are all swallowed by the water while he is standing on the roof of the house. That's what it reminded me of. It is never easy to accept the death of a loved one but it is in the course of nature that the older one dies first. And if this is reversed, one is outraged and cannot accept it. It just is not right.

After I realized that I had not lost my mind after all, I went back to sleep. Next morning brought another visitor, Mr. *Gabor.* He came rather early with a package from his wife. It was a coffeecake specially made for me. I was touched, and thanked him profusely. I still didn't have anything for him and felt pretty bad about it. But I saw and understood that he was proud he could do something for me.

"Where is your fiancé, if I may ask?"

I admitted that I didn't know and told him briefly what I did know. He sat quietly for a while in deep thought without saying a word.

"Do you know when he left?"

"That is what I don't know. All he said was that they would leave as soon as it was possible."

"Have you heard from Wallenberg perchance?"

"No, should I have? Why do you ask—Mr. *Gabor*? Do you know anything about him?"

"No, of course not. I left as soon as I could to my family and stayed a bit. They wanted to join me here, but I begged them to stay there and promised to get them once life returned to more or less normal. My wife still asked if you wouldn't like to go there for a while. She feels you could rest there and recuperate after all the hardships you have had to endure here."

"That is very alluring, but I am still in charge of the children and of course I am waiting for Oskar, but I'm very grateful."

He kept quiet a while, then raised his voice and started to talk without looking at me. That was unusual, as his was a candid straight gaze. I knew instinctively that he had something to tell me and didn't know how to begin. So I just waited. He finally started:

"A collegue of mine from the Police Force told me something that I should relate to you for what it's worth." I wondered what was coming.

"He was within sight of the vehicle that took Wallenberg. He saw that Russian soldiers escorted it. As a matter of fact, that was what caught his attention. The vehicle did not belong to the Russians, but they escorted it. It was at the time of the accident you mentioned and they were about to take Vilmos Langfelder, the chauffeur away. He overheard a fragment of a conversation between two Russians there. He was born and raised in the Northeast corner of Hungary where Russian is spoken, so he understood what those Russians on the motorcycles talked about. A fragment of their conversation was that the destination of that car had been changed by special orders. What that meant, he did not know."

He stopped talking and I just looked at him stupefied. "What could that have meant?" I asked him.

"I don't know, Miss. Didn't you say they were on their way to *Debrecen* to see General Malinovsky?"

"Yes, that was the idea. Do you suppose they took them somewhere else? Did your colleague see Oskar?"

"He didn't know the others, only Wallenberg, as he was often guarding one or the other protected houses and offices and saw Wallenberg repeatedly. He only said there were three passengers in the car, one chauffeur. One of the passengers did not return to the car after the accident, so only one stayed with Wallenberg. This person must have been your fiancé."

"Do you know which day that was?" I asked.

"I believe the seventeenth or eighteenth of January, so he said."

He got up and left soon with a promise to come and visit me again. I gave Zsuzsa this new information. She didn't understand it any better than I did. But she didn't like it and mumbled, "He shouldn't have left you here alone."

This was the first time she uttered her opinion. I said nothing, but agreed with her. Where in the world could he be, why doesn't he let me know if there was a delay? And if they took him somewhere else, not where he wanted to go, where to, and why? All this was too much for me and it made no sense whatsoever.

It was lucky that the children kept me so busy it didn't leave enough time for me to brood about Oskar's disappearance. Disappearance? I repeated this new concept to myself. Indeed. What else can you call it?

I tried to push the affair out of my mind and concentrate on the work. It was time to compose a letter to Mr. Riley to write a little bit about Rozsika. I couldn't mail it directly to America yet, but I could get it to a European country somewhere in the West and from there they could forward it. I thought first to mail it to Oskar's mother, but I declined the thought and rather decided upon Mr. Lutz, the Swiss ambassador who had been so kind to me and who had invited us with Oskar to visit him after the war was over. I had his home address. After I took care of this I felt good about starting the process of emigration for Rozsika. I didn't want to wait with it for Oskar's return, or our trip up North. It would involve a long delay. Perhaps something could be arranged from Budapest too.

It looked as if they slowly restored the most essential things and life would return, perhaps sooner than Oskar had predicted. Water, electricity, even gas was reinstalled and soon the streetcars started to work. Open markets thrived. You could buy fresh eggs, milk, cheese, produce, even poultry, oil, sugar, flour, etc., but you had to barter; no one accepted money.

Besides the *Corvin*, I once saw, shortly after the Russians took over, a grocery store, or maybe it was a dairy on *Klauzál* Square that became a collecting depot for the dead. It was piled to the ceiling with bodies. By now it had reopened to sell milk, butter, cheese, and the like. I could never enter it. Each time I went close I remembered that awful smell and sight. The impression was so strong that years later once when in Frankfurt a/M. I happened to need something from a similar store and I went to the nearby one, not far from the *Hauptbahnhof,* the main railroad station. As soon as I entered, the store "turned" itself into that one on *Klauzál* square, and I could not buy anything there. Such was the overwhelming power of my memory that I almost suffocated and rushed out of there, forgetting milk, cheese. I left even my appetite behind.

One day as I was trying to find something in the market, something special for Zsuzsa and Rozsika as a surprise, I heard my name from a distance. For a very tiny fraction of a moment I hoped it was Oskar calling" "Agi, Agi," but the voice was not his. I stopped and waited. I heard it again from nearer and looked. There were a lot of people in the market and many were taller than I am, so I could not see. Finally there he was, Dr. G. He hugged me and looked so happy, as if he had found a long-lost treasure. I was very happy to see him too. I hadn't even known if he had survived the war or where he was.

"Thank God I found you, Agi. I have been thinking of you constantly. I know, I know, you're going to say you're engaged. I am not posing any difficulty, I'm just happy to see you alive. How well you look, just a little thin. But that can be helped."

"I'm extremely glad to see you. Where were you during the darkest days? How did you manage? Will you tell me, even if not here in the marketplace?"

"May I hope that this means that you'd see me sometime and let me talk?"

"But of course. Didn't we decide to stay friends? Didn't we agree to meet after the war? Remember?"

"Yes I do, except I had no idea that I would really survive all the horrors. It was not easy." He sighed ever so lightly. "But first things come first. No more of the doctor business, I do have a first name, you know."

I laughed, "All right, Ervin, then when and where will you tell me about your odyssey?"

"I'm at your service. As for the time being I'm not working yet. My life is far from being organized, so why don't you choose place and time?"

"How about a walk in the City Park tomorrow, early afternoon?"

"That's perfect. Could I pick you up or meet you at your home, I mean your present home? No doubt you did not stay in Buda, or you wouldn't be here. The fighting is still going on over there."

I swallowed. I hadn't told him yet about not having my old home. He must have noticed the chance of expression on my face and he turned very serious.

"What is it that just crossed your mind and cast a shadow on you? What is it that you did not tell me?"

"I'm not on the couch." I tried to be lighthearted, but it didn't work. My voice broke, I breathed deeply and faced him: "Ervin, our home had a full hit before the siege started and my parents were at home. I happened to be here in Pest that day; this is how I escaped. I have been taking care of children who are without any parents. I've been living with them in a White Cross Home ever since." And I gave him the address.

"I don't know how to express my deepest sympathy, what I feel, dearest Agi. It is simply unimaginable. I can hardly accept it for a fact. I know what happened, I know how many perished, but your parents! How terrible this war is, no mercy for anyone. You darling girl, how bravely you told me." He stopped a second, then shook my hand, saying: "I won't dwell on the subject anymore. Your wound is too fresh. I'll be in front of the *Anonymus* at two thirty p.m."

"I'll be there, Ervin."

I was slightly relieved that he did not ask about Oskar's whereabouts. No doubt he would have, had I not given him that shocking information. I felt really good about having met him. He had known my parents, our home, and that created a pleasant bond between us.

I was thinking of the letter I had just managed to send to Mr. Lutz and regretted that I did not think of this before. Mr. Riley had never laid his eyes on Rozsika. Surely they would love to have a picture of her. Most likely, no, absolutely and positively surely he could not have any idea how much the child must look like him. So, I decided on the spur of the moment to go to the old studio on *Dorottya* Street, corner of *Vorosmarty* Square. It was situated on the top floor of the famed

Gerbeaud Palace. I knew by then that the parents were dead, but the son survived, to my best knowledge. How I knew that was that Wallenberg was often accompanied by him, as he was an excellent photographer.

I happened to find him home, he opened the door himself. I introduced myself, explained my connection to Wallenberg. At hearing his name, he invited me in and offered me real coffee with sugar cubes. It was incredible. He had found it somewhere in a cupboard, he explained. As we chatted, I found out that his fiancée was deported in June and he hadn't heard of her yet but he was firmly hoping for her return. He immediately agreed to make a few shots of Rozsika. He agreed to do it as soon as I wanted it. So I returned to take Rozsika and put her in her best dress, combing her carefully.

He would not accept a penny for it and I had the pictures in one day. They were lovely He made enlargements and small ones, suitable to send, also some for later use in passport and other documents. He offered to make some of me too if I needed it for anything. I thanked him. I had no idea when I might need them. It would be a long time before photographers opened their stores once again.

Rozsika was most impressed with the elegant place. "Look, Agi, the stairs are covered with leather." I hadn't noticed it until then. She was also amazed to see the large studio with the different lights and backgrounds that could be used: landscapes, elegant furniture pieces, period chairs, potted plants, a huge velvet drape. The walls of the entry were decorated with pictures. You could recognize artists, opera singers, ballet dancers, politicians including the regent, Nicholas Horthy, his daughter-in-law and the grandchild and lots of counts, countesses, and other celebrities. One particular photo caught my eyes and I stopped in front of it.

"What an exquisitely beautiful woman, doesn't she look like Ingrid Bergman?" I asked.

"Ah, that is the princess *Odeschalchi,* she is very special," he admitted. "By the way, have you heard of Wallenberg?" he asked me.

I told him what little I knew. His face grew serious.

"I don't like that a bit. It does not sound right. God knows where he is, where they took him." His face was full of worry.

He promised to deliver the pictures to me in person, as he spent very little time at home and it was sheer luck that I found him there, he said. He was too lonely there with the recent horrible events fresh in his mind. I explained what had happened to my parents.

"I'm terribly sorry for that, but that was a less cruel death," he muttered, more to himself than to me. I thought of Elli, who had expressed similar feelings.

What horrible times we must be living in that no matter how terribly people suffered and died, there were millions of others with worse fates. It seemed that no matter where I went, whom I talked to, they had a heartbreaking story behind them.

Rozsika was so excited that she had her picture taken that I had to ask her not to mention it to the other children. "We don't want to hurt their feelings, Rozsika, that you have something that they don't."

"But couldn't they have their pictures taken too?"

"I don't think I could ask the photographer again for such favor. He has enough problems of his own. You just have to accept that. I would like to do it too, but sometimes we just cannot do what we would like to."

Her more-than-mature answer came swiftly: "I know."

I hugged her and we did not talk about it anymore. But I felt an urge to write to the Rileys again to prepare them for what a precocious child they were going to have. But it was too soon after my previous letter, so I just made a mental note to bring up this incident some other time. Maybe when I send the photos, it might be appropriate.

I mentioned to Zsuzsa the evening that I was going to meet an old friend of mine. She was very interested so I told him about Ervin, how he liked me but understood that I had been engaged to Oskar. He was very sorry; before he had to return to the forced labor camp he asked me to keep in touch if possible and stay friends. I agreed.

"Did you tell him about Oskar's disappearance?" she asked. The word hit me, like a cold knife. I used the very word to myself when mulling over the recent events. So Zsuzsa also had similar impressions.

"Not yet. I told him about my parents and hearing of that tragedy he could not bring himself to ask anything. I was glad he didn't. I am confused enough. Do you know, Zsuzsa, I have a turmoil within me."

She looked at me, showing great interest, understanding, and curiosity all mixed together into a special look expressed in her face and eyes. I looked back at her and continued:

"I find myself often angry with Oskar for having left me alone. Then again I'm ashamed for my selfishness. But in all sincerity his work here was finished the minute the Russians entered the city and he just didn't know when to stop. Whatever Wallenberg and he had in mind could have been worked out once Budapest was totally free of the Germans. That's the way I see it, at least. On the other hand, since he, as you put it, 'disappeared,' and truly that is the only proper word describing the silence surrounding them, I should be worried about his whereabouts. But somehow anger overcomes this. Maybe because I don't believe that he is in danger. What trouble could the two of them be in, anyway? What did they do, if not give the most heroic and self-sacrificing help to those persecuted and downtrodden pariahs, tortured and ultimately sentenced to horrible deaths. I simply cannot imagine anyone harming them for that. If the Nazis had caught them, I would know why. But they were in Russian hands, so to speak, this is evident from what Dr. Peto told me. And he was the last person who talked to them before they vanished. In a way I blame Oskar for this. When he returns I will not admit my doubts, I would be utterly ashamed of myself, not being worthy of him. I'm sure he'd have a perfectly logical explanation why he did not get in touch with me—that it was impossible, or perhaps he tried and the message did not reach me. After all, don't we constantly hear that sporadic shots are still killing people? Or could they have been killed on the way? Perish the thought. Somehow I can't believe this."

Zsuzsa interrupted me: "Don't torture yourself, Agi. I can perfectly understand every word you are saying. You'll be able to see clearly only when he returns and explains. Until such time, just put the whole thing aside, don't torment yourself. You cannot find the answer by brooding and blaming him or yourself. And don't be so harsh on yourself. You have the right to hurt and be angry, but suspend your judgment until you know the facts."

"Thank *you*, Zsuzsa. You're a true friend. I hope someday I can do something for you too, though I don't wish that you be in such an agony and dilemma."

She laughed. "Don't you think that you have already done plenty for me and my family? Have you forgotten?"

"That isn't what I meant, Zsuzsa. I mean normal problems in normal lives."

"I know what you mean, but your problem is not part of a normal life."

"True," I mumbled." And we went to sleep.

We still shared a room; we had gotten used to each other and found comfort in talking things over quietly after each day, having spent them with the children or taking care of whatever was necessary. We had a little bit more time now for ourselves, as slowly new personnel trickled in, teaching the children, taking them to the park, and taking care of all their needs.

It was a cool, dry day. The sun shone through the still-barren branches of the trees that were slowly budding with a promise of spring. I went to the City Park in the direction of the statue of *Anonymus,* an early medieval poet who signed himself simply *Anonymus*—the one without a name—and whose real identity had never been discovered. True to this *nomen est omen,* a sculptor had recreated him sitting on a pedestal covered by ample folds of a garment that included a hood pulled down deep over his face. As his head was tilted forward and the hood fell over it, no one could see his visage. It always looked somewhat scary to me, almost representing Death, as the bronze had darkened over the years into a blackish finish.

I sniffed the crisp air and noticed a few snowflowers gently swaying in the breeze as if nodding to me in a friendly manner, almost encouraging me to go ahead and have a good time.

The Zoo was not very far, but I had heard that all the animals had perished during the siege, as nobody fed them. There wasn't enough food in the city to feed the people, let alone the animals. Poor creatures, even they suffered in this war. Only the two huge stone elephants at the entrance were intact, waiting for future live brethren to be transported there from the other end of the world. Would they tell them the story of their perished predecessors? Or would they keep mum, not to frighten them away?

As I approached *Anonymus,* I noticed Ervin pacing up and down, around the statue. I noticed that he did not wear a hat, though it was still cool; rather his light brown slightly curly hair was a little ruffled. He smoothed it the instant he noticed me. Instead of a shawl he had on a turtleneck pullover. He waved to me and hastened his steps to greet me.

"Isn't it a miracle, Agi, that we really meet again after all that has happened?" We shook hands and walked side by side. There was a certain rhythm in his stride and I fell in automatically. He took my arm and smiled at me encouragingly. It felt good, as if I belonged to someone again.

"Just as friends," he said, smiling again.

It was not the first time that I noticed that his eyes smiled on their own, before his mouth would break into a smile.

When I told about this good feeling to Zsuzsa later on, I admitted that though I belonged to Oskar, it was a pleasant feeling to have a bond with Ervin.

"I have to apologize, Agi, that I did not express my most sincere condolences to you. I was so stunned, I still can hardly believe your loss. I cannot tell you how highly I thought of your parents. You are a very lucky girl to have been born to such special people."

"Thank you, Ervin, I appreciate that. But I really told you about myself, now it's your turn to fill me in on your whereabouts since we last met."

"All right, here it is briefly: It was January 1943 and our group was ready to leave towards the front in the Ukraine. Then they delayed the departure and it was finally cancelled. The explanation: 'There is a little trouble out there, hence the delay.' We didn't know it then for sure, just suspected that the Germans were retreating, pursued by the Red Army. Lots of our comrades taken there before had perished, others managed to escape. We also knew one who drove a horse-pulled carriage all the way back and arrived in one piece. But that was the exception. For every such lucky escape there remained innumerable and unaccountable dead in unmarked graves, or many disintegrated without having a grave. The degradations were endless. To have a grave was a symbol that you were a human being once upon a time." He sighed deeply. We took a few steps in silence, then he continued:

"So, we were sent to work in a variety of camps, usually in the vicinity of Budapest. Once we stuffed salami into the casings in such unsanitary conditions that we were apalled and hoped that it was due to the war and that in normal times it was taken care of properly. At any rate, it'd be a long long time before I could eat salami again, if ever. Then we were to lift huge bales of hay in enormous sacks. I remember a youngster, small of stature and very lean, wearing huge horn-rimmed glasses. The poor fellow fainted under its weight and the rough sergeant kicked him and called him a lazy good-for-nothing so-and-so. I wonder if he survived the war; I lost track of him. Well, from here we were sent away somewhere in the country and they made us dig deep ditches. The rumor spread with the speed of lightning that they were going to line us up and execute us so that we'd fall into It. Like mass graves. We heard that similar fashions were in vogue out in between the Don, Dnieper, and Prut rivers. A lot of us believed it and fled, including myself. I have to tell you that as long as I live it'll be on my conscience that the two Jewish brigade leaders, a father and son, were executed there, as a punishment for our escape. I knew the younger man well, he was a fine, well-educated fellow. I also know his fiancée, a very charming young lady. I was ashamed to be alive. If we had known! Or would they really have shot all of us anyway?"

He stopped and I couldn't help saying, "Ervin, don't torture yourself. It is not your fault. The situation and the cruelty was responsible, not any of you who escaped."

"Thank you, Agi." After a few moment of silence he went on:

"A few of us were together. Naturally we removed our yellow armbands and hid our caps that would have indicated what we were to anyone looking at us. But we had no papers other than the true identifications. And young men on the loose might be deserters from the army. Well, we were deserters from the forced labor camp. For that they courtmartialed you. What to do? A few had addresses where they might be able to hide. If they made it or not, I don't know yet. Somebody heard of the protected houses and embassies and tried to get in. Again I don't know with what luck or result. I seriously considered going to your place and ask if I could stay there a while, but I knew the risk, what could happen to your family should they be found out, and I rejected this plan. The shooting had already started, the Russians were at the edge of Budapest, and I was not very far from this very spot here. A shot flew by me and grazed my shoulder. I felt a sharp, shooting pain and something warm covered it and my clothes stuck to it. As it was winter I could not, I did not want to take off my clothes to see what had happened. I had a pretty good guess that I had been hit and was bleeding. I had no intention of bleeding to death, or fainting in the cold all by myself. The City Park here was totally abandoned, not a living soul stirred. Agi, please don't think that I lost my mind, but I walked by the *Anonymus* and in my weak condition it seemed to nod to me in a certain direction, as if suggesting that I go that way. I walked in a daze the way he showed me and after what seemed to be an interminable time, I could make out the *Alice Weiss* building, part of that large hospital complex. I noticed that it was turned into a Red Cross Hospital, as it flew its flag. I stumbled in and fainted in the lobby. When I came to, I was in a ward all bundled up and a friendly doctor told me that I was going to be all right. I stayed there during the siege. When I recovered I offered to work for my keep. And that is where I was liberated. I could not leave for a while yet, as the fighting was fierce, as you very well experienced it. Then once the city was freed, I walked toward it, scarcely recognizing it. I was thinking of you and could hardly wait for Buda to be free too, so I might go and see you. And then, there in the marketplace I spotted you. I couldn't believe my eyes."

"I don't think our generation will find it difficult to tell our grandchildren interesting stories about our youth," I said.

"That's for sure. What a thought!"

We walked a while in silence again. Then he turned to me. "Wouldn't it be nice to be able to go to a pastry shop and order hot chocolate nice piece of cake?"

"Yeah, do you think those times will ever return?"

"I'm sure, it's only a matter of time."

"Would you like to come up and see the Home with all the children?" I asked.

"Yes, but rather some other time. I was going to suggest that you come to my place—no suspicious thoughts, please. It belongs to a friend of mine with whom we shared the place during the war. I went to school with him and he has not returned yet. I don't know just where he was taken to. I hope he'll be back. Until that time I will be alone there. I could offer you a cup of tea that was left there from the time before we left. Would you care to come for a short visit? Then I'd walk you back to the Home."

"All right, one cup of tea," I agreed.

It was a modern two-room, entry, bath, and kitchen apartment. It was furnished in half-modern, half-rustic style with Hungarian woven rugs on the floor; the wall and the table from different parts of the country. It was tasteful and simple. I was looking at the interesting collection of books while Ervin went to the kitchen to brew the tea. He served it nicely on a tray. He even had some sugar cubes. A real treat. I liked mine with milk, but that was not available as yet. He put on a record. It had been a long time since I had heard music. I sat motionless, sunk into myself and into the past. It brought back my parents, our home. I couldn't help it, tears started rolling down my face. I could not hold them back. It was overwhelming. The piece was Tchaikovsky's Second Piano concerto. It was played with such vigor and verve that finally it won me over to its beauty and I was composed by the time Ervin returned from the kitchen.

"Thanks for a lovely time, Ervin, and the tea. This place is very inviting. You're lucky that it was left intact." He went to get my coat, put on his own, and we left.

Only after we had parted did it occur to me that he did not ask about Oskar. It must have been on his mind, or did he forget? Not very likely. Perhaps he expected that I'd bring up the subject. Oh well, it'll come to it. Hopefully Oskar would be back soon. More than a month had passed since the time when Dr. Petö said that Oskar and Wallenberg had left.

XI.

I decided to go to the offices once again and see if anyone had any idea of Wallenberg's and Oskar's whereabouts. Last time I found out something quite accidentally; perhaps I'll be able to learn more this time. No such luck. They didn't know anything. They looked rather gloomy and did not think very positive thoughts about the silence enveloping the case. Then someone remembered that there was a letter addressed to me. I hastily opened it, thinking it was from Oskar or about him. It was about him all right, but not from him. His mother wrote to me from Stockholm.

> Dear Agi,
> I hope you're not offended that I call you by your first name without really knowing you, but I feel that you're no stranger. Oskar has talked about you so highly that I can hardly wait to embrace you and call you my daughter. I am also looking forward to hear you play the piano, solo or partaking in our chamber music group.
> I'm afraid I have to burden you without ever having met you with asking you to fill me in what happened to Oskar. I haven't heard from him for quite some time and I'm beginning to worry. I know that the mail might have gotten lost. Still, I feel uneasy until I have positive news. This is why I'm writing. You being in the same city most likely have some news of him if you're not together with him. Would you please fill me in on everything you know. I hope our next exchange of letters will

be free of worry and we can start then to get acquainted with each other. Until then with love,

(signed)

I realized that she had not received my thank-you note yet; otherwise she would have referred to it. About the content of this letter—hm. What was I to do? I had no intention of causing her worry. On the other hand I could not keep quiet about either my fears or the fact that no one in Budapest knew about his whereabouts. I felt I had to tell her the few facts I knew, and express my hope that before long he'd be back and everything would be clarified. I also expressed my ardent wish to meet her and put the whole war behind us. I mailed it and wondered about the result. Would I hear from Oskar soon or would she worry with me?

In the meantime people in Budapest started to tell different stories about Wallenberg. The most prevalent one was that they were taken to Russia into a prisoner-of-war camp. That certainly didn't make any sense and I couldn't believe it, nor did many others. But the fact remained that neither of them returned, nor did they arrive in *Debrecen* where they were headed. Others suggested that since at the time they left, the fighting was still fierce; they might have been simply hit by shots or, most likely, hit a mine, in which case all of them perished including the escort. Some speculated that they might have been ambushed by still-free roaming and desperate German soldiers or become the victims of Arrowcross atrocities. There was, however, no basis for any of these. Nobody knew the facts.

In view of these rumors and that Oskar was really missing, I did realize that something had gone utterly wrong. I did not know what to believe, where he was, but every day passing without news from him made me sadly aware that he passed onto a road he did not choose. The same was true of Wallenberg. Whatever happened to them, it was not what they wanted. They had either already met their Maker or, if alive, they must have been kept against their will and in a clandestine way, otherwise they would have been permitted to write. It was a terrible realization, but no matter how I tried I could not find another logical explanation. I was hoping against hope that I would still hear from him before his mother's next letter reached me.

My anger subsided, but I still felt that the two of them should have stayed put, and then none of that would have happened. I didn't write history and I could not influence it. It was merely what I thought. And for the fact that they started out in the middle of a battle still raging, I blamed him. I also started to feel terribly sorry for him, more so than for myself. It must be agonizing to be kept alive and unable to communicate.

It was Zsuzsa who straightened me out again, after I shared my doubts and feelings of uneasiness about Oskar's vanishing.

"Torturing yourself will not bring back Oskar or Wallenberg, you only hurt yourself. I can't tell you to put it out of your mind, but for heaven's sake give it time and things will sort themselves out. Try to enjoy that we have soap and water again, can breathe freely. Some day we'll find out the truth."

With that we turned the lights off and as I was about to fall asleep with Zsuzsa's words still ringing in my ears I realized that she had said something she might not even been aware of: "Someday we'll find out the truth." The question was, would Oskar and Wallenberg tell us the truth or would we only hear of it? Somehow her words indicated the latter to me. Maybe he was really dead. My God! I forced myself not to think of it. Zsuzsa was right. I couldn't solve the problem. I'd have to take care of Rozsika by myself, the sooner the better. If Oskar returns to me, we'll start a new life. If not, I'll have to do it by myself, by myself, by myself....

After a deep, deep sleep I woke up somewhat sluggish the next morning. It took me forever to get ready, not at all my custom. Zsuzsa noticed.

"Is something the matter?" Then she added as an afterthought, "I mean physically this time. You don't look so good. Perhaps you should stay in bed, Agi."

"Thanks for the concern. I feel a little under the weather, no specific complaints, though. I don't feel like staying in bed, but I somehow crave fresh air. If you don't mind, I'll take a walk this morning, will be back in no time. It'll do me good."

"Have it your way. If there is anything I can do, let me know."

I took off aimlessly and soon found myself in the State Park once again. It was not that close, but it was the closest green spot and fresh air from our location. When I lived in Buda, trees, shrubs, lawn were all over; in our yard, on the streets nearby. I didn't have to find a park. The lilac bushes used to edge the yards, perfuming whole sections, followed by roses and lilies this time of the year. Nobody planted fresh bulbs last fall in the park, so only a few crocuses and daffodils and tulips showed up instead of the profusion of colorful beds, but the forsythias bloomed. Most of them had already lost their starry little blossoms and the purple shade reigned, that is, the lilacs in all hues. They were not affected by the war and proved that nature is neutral and can outlive humans. Soon I spotted Anonymus sitting majestically and motionless, deep in thought or reverie, befitting a poet.

I was thinking of Ervin. I found it amazing that a mature man like him had had that notion that the statue actually beckoned to him and led him to the hospital's safety. I glanced up and realized that I had gone there for similar advice. Was I cracking up? I had held myself by force until now. I lost my parents; now it looked as if I might have lost Oskar too. I was all alone in the world, except for a few friends and some relations I was not very close to as they lived far away from us. I sat down on a nearby bench, just to relax.

The day was mild. The sun rays broke through the white clouds, somewhat diffusing the light and creating an unusual illumination. The folds on Anonymus' gown shone bright against the darker surface. I noticed how shiny the leaves were; so was the statue. I realized that there must have been a spring shower early that morning, bathing the stately trees: platans ashes, beeches, yews, and several century-old oaks. How long all of them had been standing there silently witnessing the folly of many generations, carefully recording all events in their inside rings. They kept vigil. A light breeze moved the leaves and cool water drops fell on my face and neck. A light shiver shook me and I dried my neck with my handkerchief. As I looked up, the statue addressed me.

He started a conversation, or rather a monologue. He seemed to mock my not overly rosy mood: "You came here for guidance? What can I say that you don't know already? Haven't you seen how dreadful men can be, what they can do to hurt and harm each other? They're beasts, most of them. Why do you state that life is worth living? You can find peace only in death. There is nothing to be afraid of. On the contrary, it gives one comfort. You don't suffer any more either from hunger, thirst, pain, or loss of loved ones. It is really a safe haven. I know you cannot deny that I'm right and you're a dreamer."

"What kind of guidance is that?" I shouted back to him quite loud. A good thing no one was around, although I didn't pay attention to that at the moment. "Of course life is worth living. All right, there was a terrible war that is coming to an end. Who knows how many perished among dreadful circumstances. But life always goes on. It is in the course of nature. All right; if I don't know why, neither does anyone else. That doesn't alter anything. And it is very much worth while living. Even if I lost my dear parents, their memory lives in me and they've shown me that life can be very beautiful and uplifting. Yes, you can help others who need it and if life is hard, there is always music and art. Those who created them also suffered, but they also brought something eternal forward that delights generations endlessly. You, as a poet should know: *'ars longa, vita brevis.'* For every mean thing one can find good and kind people; they just don't make so much noise, so it is harder to find them. But if you seek them out, there they are. All right, I agree on one point that you stated, that death is not to be feared and in certain cases it comes as a blessing. But most of the time it is better after a life lived."

"I knew you would see it my way, at least partially." I seemed to hear a slight chuckle. "Friends?" he asked.

"Yes, friends." And I got up and left.

I turned back once more and half aloud shouted back:

"Thanks, you did help me."

I felt better. As a matter of fact. I also felt life surging up in me that I had not felt for a long time. I had a lot to do. Above all and first of all to get Rozsika's affairs into the proper channels. I felt so good, I was almost ashamed of myself and a long-ago learned line came to my mind:

> "Bliss was it in that dawn to be alive
> But to be young was very Heaven!"

Even if Wordsworth referred to the French Revolution and I referred to the end of World War II, it was deeply felt. It was the first time that I felt alive and young, and I was sure that there was a future ahead, even without Oskar.

I stopped with consternation. Had I already buried him? Didn't I even mourn him, miss him, wasn't I unhappy without him? Yes. I would mourn him, I would miss him forever. But I also knew that I was deeply hurt that he had deserted me and that was an abandonment that he did twice to me. Yes twice. Through my dodanella connections I found out that in a previous life he had also abandoned me. Come to think of it, it occurred also after a war, the Great one. What did wars do to him? Lots of people who survived wars returned to a normal life. Not he. Maybe that was his great asset, his being so very refined and artistic. But did this, on the other hand, affect him in such a way that he lost his surefootedness and make him commit fatal mistakes? Witnessing so much cruelty and horror must have been the cause. One ought to help and he did, doing his utmost, no, much more than that. Was it his downfall that he wanted to go on helping, perchance? No matter. He left me and I could not forgive that. I felt the anger again, in spite of the probability that he himself was now in danger if still alive.

I never realized that I was so hard and unforgiving. Was I really? If he had returned I would have been the happiest person on earth. It was his not-returning that caused me to feel the way I did. I was sure of that. Unfortunately deep down I had more than doubts about the likelihood of his return. The silence was too deep and too much time went by. And if his mother had not been notified by him, then there was not much hope.

By the time I got back, I was in a normal frame of mind, and looked after my duties. Zsuzsa was relieved that I did not get sick and regained my normal self through the walk.

Vera came. She said she had something important to tell me in absolute secrecy.

"I only tell you because I know I can trust you with not repeating a word to anyone."

I was afraid she might tell me that she got pregnant and needed help, as she did not wish to marry that guy. But I was wrong.

"We decided to leave the country and already arranged the details. We wish to emigrate overseas in due time. It is a rather complicated plan. I didn't want to leave without telling you. Peter does not know about it and I'm not telling him. I'll simply let him know that I'm going with my mother to visit relatives in another city and will stay there a couple of weeks. This way he won't look for me and by the time he realizes that I've not returned, I'll be far away, out of his reach."

"Fantastic!" I exclaimed.

"Several of us will go and hopefully we'll meet my father, who according to the Red Cross is convalescing in the American Zone, somewhere in Bavaria. That's where we'll go for the time being."

"I'm very glad for you. You have to get away from that maniac and reunite the family. It sounds as if you'll start a whole new life. I hope we'll keep in touch. Let me know of your whereabouts. Won't you?"

"You don't really think I want to vanish. Why do you think I came here in the first place? Then I wanted to tell you that I wish with all my heart that Oskar return to you. Should that not be the case, I just know you'll manage. You'll be happy, you'll see."

"Thank you, Vera, I also wish you all the best and let's write to each other. We might meet again, who knows?" We hugged and she left.

I wondered if I would ever see her again. I heard of others who planned to leave the country. Lots of people signed up, trying to emigrate to a great variety of countries. Many new organizations popped up exclusively to help the children, orphans, lost children who had no recollection of their families, names, or addresses. Nuns let us know that they had harbored children who were now available for adoption. Offices were swarming with all sorts of people of all ages, telephones were buzzing, connections were made with foreign countries. Childless couples were hoping to get children who needed parents and a home. Piles of papers were mounting on desks, overspilling cabinets.

One day I received a letter from Mr. Riley.

Dear Miss Agi,
I wish to thank you with my wife for the letter you have written and the photos of little Rozsika. I don't know where to begin to tell you of our gratitude that you thought of that and the details you wrote about her. It is helping us to form a picture of her. My wife maintains that Rozsika is a spitting image of me, that is of my childhood pictures in the family album. We have lost our only child, as you know from our files, and we cannot have more. So Rozsika, being at least mine, already found her way to her heart. We cannot tell you of the excitement we feel and how we are waiting for the day when we can greet her in our midst, and give her a fine home, a good education, and above all our love. But we also wish to know a little about you. Are you a social worker doing her duty and much more, or is there or was there perhaps a connection between you and her poor deceased mother? Also, we have no idea if you're a young person, if you have a family of your own, what your circumstances are. I beg of you not to find it idle curiosity. There is a purpose to all these inquiries. Reading between the lines, trying to form a picture of an unknown person who writes us and tries to help us to such happiness is something that forces the imagination to recreate this person, to fill in the empty spaces. If by any chance you have in mind to emigrate, we would be more than happy to help you. So, please, feel free to ask us and write about yourself as much as possible. If for any reason you do not wish to do so, we'd understand. This is

merely to express our gratitude and desire to help if that would be welcome by you. Awaiting an answer, we remain faithfully,

Mr. & Mrs. Riley

Well, that was a warm-hearted letter. Emigration? I had never thought of it. Certainly I would wait for Oskar in spite of everything. I was mad at him, I worried about him, but I loved him and hoped for his return. It was not impossible, after all. Not impossible, I told myself sadly after a moment's brooding, but not very likely. Well, I needed time. I was going to write the Rileys a letter briefly describing my situation including waiting for my fiancé. I did not wish to explain the details. Lots of people were waiting for the return of their loved ones from concentration camps, from the front, from forced labor camps, from hiding places. At any rate, I thanked them for the offer. I also told them that I would write to them again and in the meantime I wrote some more about Rozsika. I also suggested to Rozsika to write to the Rileys. She was eager to do so and asked me to be allowed to mail it herself. She wanted to go to the Main Post Office. In her mind it was her new link with her new family somehow. I gave her the address to copy and the stamps and she felt very grown up that I let her do it.

Zsuzsa was full of good news, bubbling over with excitement. Her brother returned. They didn't even know until then that he was alive. He also had his private odyssey. They had been driven toward Austria on foot in damp, rainy, often freezing weather. They barely received food and if one of them spied a potato or turnip in the field and hurried toward it to lull his hunger pains the guard shot him instantly and with glee, cursing in the most vulgar way. The road was littered with the corpses of men who simply could not go on. They were left behind. Some of them, he said—as Zsuzsa told me—undertook the role of would-be saviors. They coaxed the older ones especially to go on and not to stop, but in certain cases they failed. It was not possible for some to endure the superhuman hardships and they succumbed willingly to death, as a relief from that horrible torture that was inflicted upon them. Each time they heard a shot most of them flinched and pulled their head into slightly raised shoulders as if to find protection. It was no use. Zsuzsa's brother and a friend of his trudging together, exhausted and totally dispirited, decided to give escape a try. What could they lose? They didn't even consider it gambling, so sure were they of what was awaiting them. No illusions. They waited for the night to descend. As darkness came early, a drizzly fog enveloped the landscape, numbing not just the sights but all sounds. They stayed behind as they had agreed ahead of time. The rear guards could not notice them for once and they lay down totally motionless, waiting for the group to go on and soon camp down for the night. As time crept slowly, no sound was heard. The two of them moved ever so slightly in the opposite direction; eventually they got up and walked, holding on to each other as they wouldn't have dared call out in case they got separated.

Zsuzsa also related to me how her brother had pointed out their feeling about time standing still and weighing down on them, completely disorienting them. They weren't even sure which direction they were headed. At long last—at least so it seemed to both of them—they started to see something darker than the rest of the darkness emerge, so to speak, not unlike the pictures in the darkroom on a piece of paper developing into a photo. They were practically touching the wall, when they were sure what they saw. It felt like wood and as they cautiously moved around it, they realized that it was the size of an outhouse. Finally they found a door that was secured with a wooden stick instead of a handle. They agreed that it must be an outhouse, except there was no odor. Maybe the cold stopped it. Still, it was puzzling. They decided to open the door.

Only one of them could fit in the doorway, with the other standing, holding the door. They could not see a thing, and although they had matches they did not dare light one. The same idea hit them: to stay there during the night. If someone came, they would be out of luck, but who would go out in such a night? They sat down, cramped. Still, it was relaxing and they fell asleep from exhaustion, leaning against each other. The raw cawing of blackbirds woke them at daybreak. Though shivering they felt a renewed energy. Before leaving that abode they shot another glance at it by the early light of dawn. The fog had lifted and they noticed that the seat was immaculately clean and they remembered while sitting on it and moving that it moved with them. They reexamined it and to their astonishment they could lift up the whole seat. Lo and behold, there was no dirt of any sort in it. Instead they noticed steps going down. They looked at each other. Where to? A trap? An escape route? It was a hard decision. To descend or not to descend? Finally they decided and took the steps one by one, ever so cautiously. They landed somewhere in the dark and stood still, trying to hear something, a clue. They lit a match; its flickering light showed a tunnel-like hall with whitewashed walls spreading ahead of them with a twist to the left. They slowly continued until they came to the turn, noticing another tunnel to the right. It was a fork. They had no idea which way to go. Should they take either of them or return whence they came from and continue on the ground outdoors? As they waited, pondering, each of them expecting the other to decide, the match went out. They took the right turn this time. In a little while they stumbled into something. They lit another match that outlined the form of a large crate, its top ajar, full of clothes. They saw a candle on the floor and lit it. By its light they saw shabby, worn garments of all sizes, most outlandish. They pulled out a large black cassock, that of a priest's, wooden shoes; there was a blue-white striped bib-overall, the kind gardeners used in the elegant manors; there was a black hat with rooster feathers, not like that of the gendarmes, but rather that of a coachman. There were old-fashioned undergarments and an assortment of shoes, all for men.

The two of them started to whisper to exchange their thoughts. First they were searching for military outfits of any sort. Not one could they find. That put them a little at ease. Could that be an escape route from a castle, a monastery, a fortress? It might have served a dozen different purposes. They decided to change their dirty, smelly clothes for some they found there, except they had to keep their jackets. It would have been too cold without them. As they were getting dressed they heard a noise in the dark and froze. Both of them stood instinctively against the wall, trying to become flush with it. They heard voices and the steps of the so-far invisible men. Were there two or three of them? Then they heard the footsteps clearly and could distinguish four steps. So there were two of them. Zsuzsa's brother and the friend realized that if attacked or cornered, they would have to fight for their lives, even if they would have to kill those two unknowns. Neither of them had ever done anything like it and they awaited the confrontation with mounting apprehension.

Soon they heard their conversation clearly: "We have to be very careful with *Miklós*, we still don't know on whose side he is; luckily we have a few days now before we return. By that time the situation will become clearer."

The two men brushed by them and vanished without giving any sign that they were aware of anyone else being present or that anyone had overheard them. The two of them, hugging the wall, listened to the receeding steps and heaved a sigh when silence reigned again. They changed their clothes hurriedly, hiding the yellow armband and telltale cap in their pockets. They did not wish to leave any trace behind them. They decided quickly to resurface in these neutral garments and try their luck outside.

A cold but dry day greeted them. They felt a new energy, having slept several hours. Also the hope of escape, if tinged with uncertainty, refueled their young blood. They almost felt like boys again, playing cops and robbers. Except for the stakes; they were real. And they knew it. Luckily, they knew from which way they had approached that outhouse, so they continued in the opposite direction, which was eastbound. Their aim was to reach Budapest. How far away they were they did not know. Suddenly they heard a shrill whistle, that of a train. Train stations were always dangerous. Both the police and the military were ever-present and were likely to ask for papers, especially from young men who were supposed to be fighting on the front. They had to avoid the station at all cost. Still they found it important to find out where exactly they were and a train station would certainly display the name of the place. But as hard as they looked, they saw no houses anywhere. They slowly realized that there was no train station nearby at all. The train merely whistled. Maybe it turned a sharp curve or whatever other reason they do it for."

"Zsuzsa, this is simply fantastic." I interrupted her. "You must have memorized your brother's story."

"Agi, this is only the beginning of his story. He went on for hours and added that the two of them were going to make notes, to keep it fresh in memory and later on they would write it down in form of a book."

"I'm sure I'll be among the first ones to read it."

"You see, Agi, they went through so many adventures that old Dumas couldn't think up more. A series of lucky encounters helped them along the way. It had to be lucky, or else he wouldn't be alive to tell his story. All those poor devils who did not come back must have faced horrible people and come across insurmountable obstacles. And they certainly cannot tell their stories and someone should gather them in the form of an anthology. It should be edited for the memory of those perished."

XII.

A few words about Rozsika. She received the proper papers from the Rileys and was escorted by a Swiss Red Cross nurse all the way to Seattle, at the expense of the Rileys. They did not dare take any chances after they found out that I was not going to accompany her. Rozsika was most anxious for me to go along with her to the new land and to her new parents, but she finally accepted that I wished to wait for Oskar a little longer. I promised I would follow in due time. Rozsika also studied English and had acquired a very good preliminary knowledge by the time she departed.

 The first letter I received from the Rileys after her arrival told me that when they had their first meal together in their home, Rozsika didn't fail to ask them if they had perchance accumulated all their ration cards and saved them to have enough food for her too. She also admitted to them that never in her life had she seen a table loaded with so much food and asked that if she ate all she wanted, would there be enough left for them. I can just imagine the Rileys' emotions. By now, when I'm writing these lines, Rozsika is married and has a little girl of her own. The Rileys are still around, doting on her. There is one happy ending to a life started out with dismal hopes.

 While still in Budapest, I exchanged a few letters with Oskar's mother. I thought of returning her gift, but that would have indicated that I had given up on Oskar's return. Maybe I had by that time. After all, more than a year had gone by since his disappearance. She wrote to me on and off, telling me that both she and the Wallenberg family were trying to find out from the Russian government the whereabouts of their sons, alas with no result. There were contradictory news. Some stated that they never heard of him, others said they saw him in such and such camp. But he was nowhere to be found. It was bewildering. If the famous Wallenberg family got nowhere and was evidently lied to, what could I expect to find of Oskar's whereabouts? Were they together? Or had they been separated? Were they alive?

One day I received another letter from Oskar's mother:

Stockholm

My Dearest Agi,
I'm writing you these lines with a sad heart. No, I haven't found out anything about my son. Neither is anything known of Raoul. But I have a feeling that I should share with you. I want nothing more in my life than to see my dear Oskar again and see the two of you united. Still, I think I have no right to hold you to your promise to my son. I just can't see another young life wasted. Who knows what the future holds. I want you to feel free to start a life of your own, not waiting any longer for Oskar. You won't be young forever and I know you're by yourself, no family. I think it would be time that you started your own life while you're still young. Don't wither away. I'd only ask you to give me a permanent address where I could reach you, should Oskar return and wish to get in touch with you. Also, please keep the heirloom as a memento of Oskar. I wish you all the happiness you so much deserve.

As ever

(signed.)

I shed a few tears over this poor mother. What a considerate, brave soul. She must have given up or she wouldn't have expressed herself thus. I showed the letter to Zsuzsa. She agreed with me and shared the same opinion.

"What next?" asked Zsuzsa, point-blank.

"I don't know yet," I answered. But the wheels of the thinking machine started to creak, slowly putting into motion thoughts that were suppressed and surfaced now to outline the future. My future. What was in it? I didn't know.

Zsuzsa started to date a friend of her brother's and they were serious about each other. Zsuzsa's brother, on the other hand, seemed interested in me, but I was not ready to date anyone. I went out occasionally, but strictly on a friendly basis. I was still waiting to see if Oskar might not return from wherever he was.

Times and circumstances changed slowly. An incredible inflation swept the country that eventually outdid the hitherto most fantastic one in history, that in Germany after World War I. The Hungarian currency, the pengö, was losing its value by the hour. People who had been paid in the morning rushed to spend it, or else they would get for the same amount only half of the merchandise by the afternoon. Nobody wanted money, they all preferred to exchange goods. One U.S. dollar was enough to live on for one month when exchanged for millions of pengoes; this was also the equivalent of one kilo (two pounds) sugar, which was almost impossible to obtain.

I had my papers from the Rileys, but I should have left with Rozsika. Since I put it off for too long the papers were no longer valid, or so they informed me. Ervin, whom I seen occasionally, did not wish to tell me what to do but one day he confronted me in a very serious and I'm sure unselfish tone.

"Agi, what I'm telling you is only for your ears. Don't repeat it to anyone, please. I have a very close and trustworthy friend who has access to information that people here don't have. Neither the press nor any other forum speaks about it. The Russians are going to stay here and take full power and oppress every opposition. There won't be any freedom anymore to move or criticize anything. If you have in mind to go to America and you're only waiting because of Oskar, do it now before it's too late. It won't be possible or only with a lot of difficulty later on. I'm also leaving.

"I decided that I'd like to live my life in the free world. I saw enough of a totalitarian state already. And though this is totally different, its framework is the same. I know you're indifferent to politics and wish to live your own life, but most likely that won't be very easy here in the future. It would be better for you to leave as soon as possible. You can wait for Oskar in America too. You have his mother's address, that's all you need."

I thanked him for his solicitousness and promised to think about it. I did and I accepted his advice. The problem was that even after I tried I could not get the papers anymore. I was told to start all over, to sign up for the Hungarian Quota and wait about ten years. That sounded like a bad joke. But I realized that they did not joke. I turned to Ervin again and he had a plan for me.

He had connections and could arrange an illegal exit from the country for both of us. I didn't ask for much detail. I just followed his instructions. I trusted him implicitly and did not regret it. In a few weeks, actually some two months later I found myself in the American Sector in Vienna and three days later in a so-called Displaced Persons' camp in *Einring* near the *Stauffen* mountain, right on the border of Austria and Germany, specifically Bavaria.

The organization arranging for this emigration was rapidly spreading. As the grip of the Soviet Union took larger and firmer hold on a great number of countries, so the mass exodus started. In the camp where I stayed then, located in Bavaria, a daily trainload of people arrived from every possible country. You heard every language spoken there.

We lived in wooden barracks. They said that they had been occupied during the war by workers of the Third Reich, who were building airports. On the other hand, it might have been used for something else. What exactly, we didn't know. There was a huge field nearby with nothing sown in it but fresh earth smelling of the dead. Someone said that maybe a chemical factory's outlet was there. But one day someone spotted a wooden shoe and recognized it as those having been worn by inmates of concentration camps. So he concluded that the large field out there might be a mass grave. To this day I don't know. I never went that way again. Only an occasional wind blowing from there carrying the tell-tale stench reminded me of it.

I was hired by the camp school to teach English. For payment I received my own room and an extra package of food and cigarettes. These latter ones I sold, as I did not smoke.

Ervin departed for Paris rather soon to continue his studies in a specialized field before going to the States.

I was not very happy in that camp and there didn't seem to be any chance to get away from there. I went to the proper authorities in Munich; I talked to this and that with no result.

Many people in the camps were engaged in the black market and they prospered. I was not interested in that. I wanted to get out of that trap. I wrote to Ervin. He suggested that maybe I would be luckier to try to emigrate from Paris. I gave it a thought and tried to get entry from the French Consulate in the French Zone. I was not successful. I became desperate. Eventually I found the right connection in Ulm. There was a small group of people who could take me over—again illegally—to France. Ervin wrote that once there I could be legalized. He'd help me. He also cautioned me to be careful.

I wished Zsuzsa were with me. I would have needed her sober, matter-of-fact point of view, and also her laughter. I was alone now, trying to settle a delicate operation. I found the people who dealt in smuggling me over to France, but I dared not go alone with the guide. He seemed decent, but I was not going to take such chances. The trip involved crossing the border at night on foot. I decided to get some companions. I knew a very young couple who were anxious to go to Paris, but didn't know how. I also knew that they could pay. I returned to Stuttgart, where I was staying at that time, and informed them of the opportunity. They were delighted and came back with me to Ulm.

The day was set and the four of us started on our trip. We had passes to cross into the French Zone and landed in Saarbrücken. This town happened to be bilingual, as it kept changing hands after every war. Once it was part of France, once again part of Germany. So the population was fluent in both, the same way as *Elsas Lotharingia* was with the old city of Strassburg or Strasbourg.

Our guide suggested an excellent and bright idea, that we cross over the weekend, which happened to be a double holiday, a three-day weekend. It was toward the end of May, Whitsunday and Whit-Monday, a religious holiday in France. In his opinion there were going to be fewer raids and less document-checking, still frequent in those postwar days. We had to spend one night in Saarbruecken proper. We found a so-called *bunker* hotel that was built totally underground for safety during the war. It was so deep down that after descending all those steps, one felt the different atmosphere pressing on one's chest. The air felt damp, although outside it was a glorious and balmy spring day. We were hungry and decided to go to a restaurant. I happened to be in the restroom when the military police checked everybody's papers. So I missed that. I was glad of it. I'm not a very good actress, to put it mildly, and perhaps my behavior might have given away our clandestine plans.

Accordingly we decided to go out in the country, or to pretend to do so, as young people having an outing and picnic, taking a trip on the weekend. We knew by then that the French border was beyond the Saarbruecken cemetery at the very edge of the city. We took the streetcar to the end station and got out, climbing up the steep hill behind the cemetery. We had to stay there some two-three hours idling away, waiting for nothing else but darkness to descend. Under its protecting covers we planned to run down and cross into France, hopefully undetected by the guards. So far so good. We sat down and chatted lightly, all the time keeping an eye on the guards who were pacing up and down on the French side of the border. There were two of them. They walked in an L shape away from each other and back again, meeting and parting where the two lines of the L met. We figured we had to run down and across the railroad tracks when they started parting from each other with their backs towards us.

As it grew darker the lights of Forbach—the name of the tiny town below us already on French soil—lit up. I had a special problem. I had just managed to get a pair of brand-new most comfortable walking shoes, but they creaked. We heard the steps of the guards, so our guide concluded they would hear my steps, rather my creaking shoes as well. There was simply nothing else to do but to remove them, hang them on my neck by their shoelaces, and walk in my stockinged feet. That was far from pleasant. I never liked to walk barefoot and my knee-highs didn't protect me from the rough terrain. I had no choice, so I had to bear my extra burden in silence. But when do things go smoothly? In the middle of our descent a tremendous explosion followed by a reddish illumination of the sky knocked us down to the ground. We felt and acted as soldiers do when suddenly attacked by bullets or caught in an air raid out in the field. We could not figure out what caused it and waited bewildered on the ground to see what would follow. As it got quiet and darkness returned to the sky, we got up from that dangerous exposed area and ran as we had never run before, all the way across the tracks, into the little town's dark streets. Only a few lights shone, no sound, but our own heartbeat was heard. Then as we stopped to catch our breath, did we realize that we were not caught by the guards after all, that we had actually made it, and we were really in France.

We found out soon that the mines in Saarbrücken worked even during the holidays and hence came the occasional roar of detonation causing that incredible red and menacing illumination across the darkened sky.

As we stood there in a strange street of a strange town in a country we'd never been in before, wondering what steps to take next, soft music trickled into our consciousness. Our guide concluded logically that somewhere they must be still celebrating. It was way past midnight. We headed in the direction where the music came from and we found an open inn. We decided that the young couple with our belongings would wait in the dark for us while the guide and myself went into the inn. To all appearances we looked like any ordinary young couple while in reality we were trying to find a solution for how to get to the train and to Paris.

How much one's personality influences our actions and eventually our lives. Our guide didn't speak any other language but Hungarian. Still, with me being the spokesperson he organized and carried it all through. We ordered beer. I hate even the smell of it, so I just pretended to drink, it while B. was looking around slowly from behind his glass in order to sum up the situation. He whispered to me soon that he had spotted the owner without the shadow of a doubt. How? I don't even try to guess. He was a middle-aged man, I thought, as I looked at him. I saw him speak to this or that person, occasionally sitting down to chat with them.

"Call him to our table, Agi. Tell him we'd like to ask him something."

I addressed him in French and he immediately followed me and sat down opposite B. He turned to me asking if I spoke German. When I said yes, he continued in German asking what we really wanted from him.

"We'd like to get a car to get us to the Paris Express." He scratched his head and looked at us a while. Then he asked us, "What kind of passports or papers do you have?"

"We don't have any. We're refugees from Hungary and would like to get, with another couple who is waiting for us outside, to Paris. Do you think you could help us?"

"*Ja, ja.* I do have a small truck and could take you to Metz, the next larger city. You couldn't possibly get on the train here. This is a border town and they would ask you for documents. We should go during the night, less chance for interference here in the country. Would that be agreeable?"

We both nodded. Then he went on:

"Don't stay at the railroad station waiting for the express to come. Buy your tickets and proceed instantly to the proper platform where the Paris Express would come. Make sure that you're on the right place."

This was important in order to avoid both the military and the police asking for papers. Then he asked us how much money we could pay. We said we'd prefer to pay in goods.

"What kind of goods do you have?" he asked with interest.

"Real cocoa, Hersheys, Nescafé in small cans, milk powder, called Klim, which is milk backwards." When I said this, B. looked at me and laughed. He had never thought of that, while I was in the habit of liking to read backwards. The Frenchman also laughed when he found out what was so hilarious.

"Anything else?" he asked businesslike.

"Yes, assorted jams, Spam, and sardines."

"Regular black-market?" he laughed.

"Not really," I said, looking at him quite innocently and sincerely. "We saved them from the packages we got."

"I see." He smiled. "I accept."

We heaved a sigh. I had no idea what he thought of who we were, but at that point I really didn't care. He left to fill up his truck and we went to tell the couple the good news. We were to meet in ten minutes behind the inn.

We paid B, who returned to Germany on foot through the woods during the cloak of the night, and perhaps he helped some other people to cross the border. He didn't seem to have any special aim in life, so he told us. He just lived from one day to the other. So did we, never knowing what the next day would bring, especially when we tempted fate with these illegal crossings. But we did have an aim. We wanted to establish a regular—if you wish—bourgeois existence and live like humans used to before the world caught fire and the war uprooted so many who were without homes, without loved ones. We tried to find a new ground where we could grow new roots and get acclimatized.

We found the truck in the dark, climbed into the back of it, and put down our belongings. He started the engine, which purred in a somewhat promising manner. He drove over dark and bumpy back roads. We trusted that he knew what he was doing. He let us out near the railroad station in Metz in the early morning hours and wished us good luck. We all watched him pull out and disappear in a cloud of dust.

"*Trois billets pour Paris, s'il vous plaît,*" I heard myself say at the ticket office in Metz and I handed over the prepurchased francs to pay with. It was the first time in my life that I tried to speak French (other than to the innkeeper, who, however, turned to German instantly) and I hoped they'd understand me. They did, and I took the three precious pieces of paper into my hand and gave two to the couple. Immediately after this we went down the subway stairs to the platform where the Paris Express was to arrive. People of all sorts were coming and going on the opposite side as well as in the tunnel. We ourselves had a hard time staying together on account of the swarming travelers. When we reached the place where we were supposed to wait we put down our belongings and sat on them or walked up and down a little. We had almost two hours before the train was due. Any time a uniform of any sort approached, I powdered my nose in order to hide, so to speak. No one paid any attention to us.

Finally the Express pulled in. It was on time. It was already full and we had a rather hard time boarding. Like sardines. We managed to put our luggage down in the hallway and sat down on them. We were wondering who was staying home. Everybody seemed to be packed onto that one train. Was the whole world going to Paris?

In a few hours we arrived at the *Gare de l'Est*. We knew by heart which way to go to get to the right Metro station. I bought the tickets again and we got to the address we had memorized.

It was almost incredible how smoothly our trip turned out. Nobody as much as looked at us. Nobody cared who we were. We saw in that Metro a black man. He might have come from the French colonies. We also spotted a colorfully dressed figure with a blue turban wrapped around his head. Perhaps from India? Well, this was Paris and you saw every nationality under the sun. I had never seen either black men or people from India before, nor Orientals, who were also visible later on the streets of Paris. It took me a long time to distinguish between a Japanese and a Chinese, not to mention other Orientals.

We emerged from the Metro at the designated station, called *Simplon,* and proceeded on foot until we reached the house where the couple's relatives lived. They were very friendly to me too; they couldn't ask enough about our trip, about life in the Displaced Persons' Camps, the sorrow they expressed about the losses we all suffered. They served us coffee, milk, and an old-fashioned Hungarian *kuglof*, a delicious coffee cake. We enjoyed it tremendously, but sitting in such comfort in a peaceful atmosphere made us realize how exhausted we really were—not so much physically as from the anticipated agony that we might not make it. We were given separate rooms, those of their grown children who were not home at the moment. It felt almost luxurious to find myself in a clean bed in a private apartment, no more barracks and dust or mud between them, depending on the weather. I felt I had returned to civilization.

The next day I got in touch with Ervin, who rushed over. I was never so happy to see anyone in my life. I was alone in a strange country, in Paris, with just a vague notion that from there I wanted to emigrate to America. What to do in the meantime was a big blank.

Ervin proved to be a pillar of strength and help, the most decent person I have ever had the good luck to meet. Totally discreet, never asking delicate questions, just helping and finding out what was to my liking, what was not. First of all he found a comfortable and reasonable hotel room for me. Everybody who was not an original Parisian seemed to live in hotels. I had never seen so many of them. Every street had its good share, elegant districts as well as modest ones.

The place he found for me was not far from Ervin's hotel. He was very thoughtful in that he did not settle me in the same hotel where he resided. He knew me well. Then he showed me a modest little restaurant and introduced me to the markets that were open three times a week in the morning hours. If one needed something in between there were the stores. He showed me what I could buy, take home with me, and eat in my room at a fraction of the cost of eating out. He proved to be very frugal and self-sufficient.

There were the bakeries. I found French bread absolutely superb when fresh. I especially liked the so-called *baguette*. Its crispness was a treat with a dab of butter spread on it.

I also had to register with the Police Headquarters at the *Cité*, the island on the Seine, close to where the Notre Dame cathedral is. I only had a first glimpse of everything, as the official papers had to be taken care of before anything else. I also got my *Carte d'Identité* and ration cards. Then Ervin taught me what kind of tickets to buy for the Metro by the week or at least in a small booklet, instead of individual tickets. That was also saving. I was absolutely fascinated by the maps in the Metro stations where one could push a button on the board under the map and the whole picture showing all the streets of Paris would light up in colorful dots outlining the route one had to take in order to get to the chosen destination. It also showed clearly where the transfer to another Metro line ought to take place.

Ervin proved to be a one-man guide, parent, friend, teacher and companion. He even bought us tickets to the Opera. He knew how much that would mean to me. We saw Gounod's *Faust* in a superb performance. We sat in a box but not down where they cost a fortune; there was a row of them on the fifth floor, facing the stage. Acoustics were good and I didn't miss seeing the singers' faces very closely. The ballet was a lovely show in itself. We went there quite often and saw among others a lot of French operas that were not performed in Budapest. The tickets did barely cost more than a good one, let's say, in the Gaumont Palace, one of the larger cinemas. Within a few days he took me all over Paris. We walked along the Champs Elysées from the Arc de Triomphe to the Place de la Concorde. Another time we walked through the maze of streets in the Montmartre up to the Sacré Coeur, feeding the pigeons and drinking in the atmosphere. Sidewalk painters and musicians crowded the streets. There weren't many tourists around in those days.

I found out that butter, chocolate, and some other items were still rationed but after Budapest I found it all abundant. Especially the big department stores, *Lafayette, Printemps, Les Quatres Seasons*. Then there were a great number of chic stores with very French clothes. The styles bespoke a very special French taste different from any other nation's. I especially enjoyed walking along the quais of the Seine. Browsing at the *bouquinists* was lots of fun. They didn't have just books, but unique postcards and memorabilia from the famous. I think this latter one was a hoax. They could not prove that Hemingway or Oscar Wilde owned it, as it was not written into them. But I guess there are always those who buy them and cherish them and believe what they are told.

It was all a dream. But I had to think of taking care of my affairs. I went to the emigration offices as well as to the American Consulate. I couldn't even get in without an appointment. They advised me that I had to go through the regular emigration channels. And so it started. A slow, tedious red tape with no time-limit in sight.

I sat down to write a letter to the Rileys, telling them that I lived in Paris now and would like to ask for their help to get to the States.

The first Sunday Ervin took me to the Louvre. Entrance was free that day as well as on Thursdays when the French children have no school and could visit the museums. I was especially awed by the Greek statues. They were perfection in marble. Then I was most astonished how small the Mona Lisa was. Its fame evidently made me think of it as a huge painting. There was so much there, whole rooms full of, just to name a few, Van Dyck, Rubens, Delacroix. I had to return there often; this time it was just a brief smorgasbord. Later on I would return and choose and enjoy just as much or as little as I could take in at one time.

I forgot to mention my first encounter with the French toilets. When I first asked where it was in the apartment where we arrived in Paris after having crossed the border, they sent me down. I found the door they pointed at and I opened it. Immediately after that I closed it. It was not a toilet. They must have misunderstood me. I had no idea what it could have been. To my astonishment they all burst out laughing. I looked at them quite bewildered, if perchance they had all lost their minds at the same time. I failed to see what was so hilarious. They stopped laughing and then came the explanation:

"Yes, it is the toilet. We didn't misunderstand you, you just didn't recognize it as it is so different from a normal toilet. You see V.D. was so rampant in the previous century in Paris that they built these odd places, a porcelain floor with a hole and two slightly raised foot-shaped places for one's shoes to stand over the hole. Using it this way there was no contact and you could not pick up any undesirable bacteria."

I smiled a strained smile. I did not find it overly amusing and returned reluctantly to the same place. Another shock awaited me upon coming out of there. When I flushed, I had to jump out of there in a hurry or I would have been splashed. I shut the door in a hurry. Who would think of such when one reads abroad of the city of light?

Since it became clear to me that I wouldn't be able to emigrate overnight, I had to find some kind of solution as to how to support myself. I found out that they taught emigrants sewing in three months, then guaranteed a job somewhere. Even while I would be learning they would pay a minimum wage that would cover my hotel room and meager food plus Metro tickets. I made a fast calculation and signed up for it.

I cannot say that I was ever fond of sewing. Far from it. But this was necessity with a capital N. So I went. It turned out that the place was run by Poles. That didn't bother me. They spoke French mostly. They put me to the machine and taught me first how to sew a straight line. Eventually we learned how to put together a man's shirt and pajamas. Someone else did the cutting. Well, to sum up the situation I wasn't very skillful, to put it mildly, and they noticed that soon. So out of sheer good will they sat me down to a buttonhole-making machine that I learned to handle rather fast. It had an intricate multi-multi threading system that somehow I acquired very easily and so that's what I was doing there. When I was through, I ironed the shirts and pajamas that the other girls finished so swiftly and beautifully. The three months passed.

But already at the beginning I had another incident with the toilet. This sewing school was on the sixth floor of a very old building in the heart of Paris. There was only one toilet for us and it was down in the courtyard. The very first time I entered it, I spotted a dead rat lying there. I jumped out of there as fast as I could and shut the door behind me, and never again did I go close to it. And I was there from nine in the morning till six in the evening! Luckily I was young and healthy and could afford such unhealthy habits.

Well, the promised job found me in the sewing shop of the famed *Galeries Lafayette*. Never did it occur to me that I'd be part of such a place. It was stepping back practically to the times of Dickens, or if not that far, then to the infamous New York sweatshops at the end of the last century and the beginning of this one. Well, we were not exactly locked in, but the ambiance was similar. There was a huge room, more like a hall. Sewing machine next to sewing machine in several rows filled most of the place. A few French girls, and mostly foreigners, were whirring away on them with the speed of light; the garment pieces becoming one solid piece under their deft fingers. In the front of the room, as on a stage, was a huge ironing board with two sections, the large for the coats and the small for the sleeves. There stood a balding man on a small dais that was attached to the ironing boards. This is how it worked. He jumped on that dais and puff, the steam poured out of the boards, pressing the garments to perfection. He worked fast, like everyone else. His jumping movements reminded me of Victor Hugo's *Le Jongleur du Notre Dame*, except that this jongleur did not do it to praise God but to earn his living. The steamed garments had a sourish smell and I noticed when going by that man that he too exuded this same odor.

We were paid by the number of garments we had finished. Every piece was numbered and you kept half of the ticket, indicating the same number that was attached to the finished piece. I ended up having to undo every single work I stitched together. The seam was all crooked, unacceptable. Next to me sat another one of the Polish refugees. She saw my desperation and suggested I slow down. Even this didn't help me.

When the bell rang at noon, starting the half-hour lunch period, all the girls jumped up and rushed like maniacs to another room with a long table with chairs around it. There they ate the lunch they had brought with them from home. It looked like a stampede and I instinctively stayed back, taking my time. I hate to rush and push. I found out the reason for this rush when I had to eat standing up. There weren't enough chairs around and they hated to eat standing.

Well, I lasted there two whole weeks. It seemed more like two hundred years. I kept looking at the wall clock. When would six o'clock come? I realized that I couldn't stay there. I never earned anything and suffered from it terribly. What next?

I conferred with Ervin and when he found out that I could type, he suggested I go to the Emigration agencies and apply for an office job. I went. I kind of prepared ahead of time what I was going to say in English. It was easier to read and write than speak that language that I had never really heard spoken. So, with trembling knees I mustered enough courage to go in and ask for a job. The lady—an American—

was rather kind and told me to go down and see a man who would give me a typing test. "If he finds you all right, you're in."

I walked down the stairs, repeating the same speech to myself slowly, in English, and entered the room. Monsieur K. interrupted me instantly when he heard me speak English.

"*Sprechen sie Deutsch?*"

"*Ja,*" was my answer.

It turned out he wasn't very fluent either and preferred someone with whom he could talk in his native language. He made me type and I got the job. What a relief that was. Again the room where I was typing was full of people from all countries. All the paperwork was done in English; the speaking varied, mostly French.

At least my financial worries were over for the time being. After a few months I got a better position and somewhat more salary. It made me feel good after that sewing fiasco.

Of course Paris was only a waystation in the course of my life, as my definite aim was to go to the States and start life anew there.

I have to admit that Paris was a beautiful "station" and I enjoyed whatever I could to the hilt, mostly in Ervin's company. The time was approaching for Ervin's departure for the States.

One beautiful Saturday we went to the *Parc Zoologique* by the *Bois de Vincennes*. Ervin rented a canoe and paddled away with me under the soft French trees, shrubs barely moving in a light breeze. It almost created the illusion that all the movement took place in the rythm of Debussy's "En Bateau." I almost heard the melody. He must have conceived it in similar surroundings.

After a while, when we were away from the crowd, Ervin stopped, and we just sat in the boat, swaying with it on top of the waves.

"Agi, how would you like to come with me to America as my wife?"

I was speechless. I looked at him with wide eyes.

"Ervin, you're not serious. I know I'm a good friend of yours and you're my best friend, but you don't bring sacrifices to a friend!"

"It is no sacrifice, dearest Agi. I love you. I never stopped loving you, I just stopped talking about it as per our agreement. Remember?"

"Well, I do like you, I even love you, Ervin. I always look forward to meeting you and am never disappointed. On the contrary. I always have a wonderful time with you. I really dread the day when you leave and I'll stay all alone. But all this should not influence one. This is no basis for a marriage."

"I don't know what else is? You admit you love me and you have a good time with me. What else can a guy hope for?"

"All this is true. Still I'm not in love with you."

He kept silent for a while and I kept pondering—was I making a big mistake? But everything I said was just the way I felt it.

"Could it be," he asked me, "that you're still attached to Oskar emotionally?"

"I'll always have a soft spot for his memory. But memory it is. I cannot imagine that he's alive when he did not at least let his mother know of his whereabouts."

"Well, Agi, I'm leaving. You have the address where you can reach me. Let's keep in touch and should you change your mind, I'll start the procedure."

We left it at that and the day came and he was really gone.

I expected to be lonely, but it was something awful. What did I want from life anyway? Was I a dreamer, a hopeless one at that? I couldn't help myself. I wanted to be in love with the man I was going to marry.

An unexpected opportunity presented itself some months later. There was a possibility to emigrate to Canada from Italy. How? As a domestic. For one year I would have to work in that capacity. After that I would be free to do as I pleased. Wonderful, I thought. I certainly could do that and it would be much easier to go over to the Rileys from Canada after the year was over.

I left Paris for Rome. After having taken care of all the paperwork in the Rome Emigration offices I was sent to a camp in Bagnoli, close to Naples. After several interviews and physical examinations I had to report to the Canadian Embassy in *Rome*. I believe it was close to the beautiful park *Gianniccolo*.

Just a word of my interview in there. Never in my life have I met such a two-faced, ill-at-ease employee at any embassy, and I have been to a number of them. He would not look straight at me, but at some invisible spot behind me. It made me feel creepy. What was the matter with him anyway? Well, I was rejected. But why? I was healthy, young, I could work like a horse, furthermore I was more than willing to do so and was most anxious to emigrate overseas. Upon my—I'm afraid rather insistent—questioning he mumbled something that I did not look like a domestic, rather like a lady, and they wanted real domestics. I was furious, but there was nothing I could do. He had the veto power, I had none.

Meanwhile I rented a room in Rome from a Hungarian family. I obtained their name and address from the emigration agency. They were very helpful and tried to make life easier for the refugees. By sheer coincidence I ran into an employee there who happened to have been in my English class in the D.P. camp in Bavaria. Upon finding out my situation she suggested a good position that had just been vacated. She got me the interview and I was promptly hired with a very adequate salary.

There I was again. I took care of myself, I had Rome to explore, alas without Ervin. I missed him more and more. I could have returned to Paris and have my old job back, but as long as I found a good one in Rome, I preferred to stay there until I could take care of my final emigration. After all, that was my aim. The more time went by the more I realized what a mistake I made when I did not go along with Rozsika. But no crying over spilled milk. I tried to make the best of it. After all, how many art-loving people have the chance to live in Rome, not just visit it once in a lifetime as tourists? In due time I knew Rome very well and I could return to my favorite spots as many times as I wished to. This was the beauty of it. A real luxury. I went back to see *Moses* or the *Pièta* who knows how many times. They became old friends. Then there were the innumerable fountains, many by Bernini. The *Tritone* fountain on the *Piazza Barberini* became my daily company as I had to walk by it on my way to work. It never failed. The minute I glanced at it and heard the trickling water, the *Triton* seemed to blow his horn loud, and I heard Respighi's music I was always so fond of. So were Respighi's *Pines* beckoning to me, the closed and open umbrellas, so typical of the local landscape. The Colosseum and the Roman Forum or rather its ruins gave one a good idea how advanced the Romans were in their time, not to mention the viaducts that provided them with running water at a time when most people lived almost like the cavemen or if better, certainly not half as clean as the Romans must have been. They leaned on slavery; so did the others, they just called them vassals, as in the Middle Ages.

I was lucky enough to be able to visit Florence, or *Firenze*, as I preferred to call it by its Italian name. I've "known" the city from my parents' books and the collection of pictures they had brought back from their honeymoon, which they spent there and in Venice. Nevertheless I didn't expect anything like it.

The Renaissance is living there and I wouldn't have been a bit suprised if Leonardo, Michelangelo, or Botticelli or for that matter any of the Medicis would have turned the corner and greeted me. I almost expected them to show up. They just about did. Their memory inhabits the city and has stamped it for all times to come.

The green and white marble cathedral with the Giotto *Campanile* vies with the *Porta del Paradiso* by Ghiberti. The riches to be found in that city are unimaginable and unexplorable. It would take a lifetime or two to thoroughly study everything there. Then to think that the famous *Ponte Vecchio* (old bridge) was already there and called the same in Michelangelo's times! I couldn't get enough of it. It is a fountain one wishes to drink from again and again.

My work got quite interesting. I was a social worker there in charge of the so called hard-core cases. They consisted of older people who had left their own country, fleeing from the Communists. They had no means and unfortunately no chance for a pleasant future. They might have been better off if they had stayed put. They obtained some meager help from the United Nations' funds but it was evident that this help was of a temporary nature. No country wanted to take in older people, they all wanted the young ones who could work and become useful and self-supporting citizens. The local economy could not absorb them either. Post-war Italy was poor. It was a pity to watch these neglected souls hope to get out of there and emigrate into a more fortunate country overseas. They refused to accept the fact that all doors were closed for them.

I was given a car and a chauffeur two-three times a week, to pay surprise visits to those who received money regularly. My task was to establish as closely as possible the fact that they were indeed in need. When these people came to our offices for interviews, they—so the gossip went—put on their worst-looking clothes to impress upon us their poverty and need. So it had been decided to go unannounced to their living quarters that might bespeak a different state of financial affairs. There were very few exceptions, however. I have seen some tasteful, if very simple abodes and also rather shabby quarters. One old woman, she must have been close to seventy, had a tiny room with a gas burner for cooking and heating water. She had no private bathroom of any sort. I believe she shared a toilet in that house with other tenants. She only spoke Polish and Italian. I only understood a little Italian, I could not speak it really, only for the most necessary things. But her poverty spoke eloquently in any language. I didn't need to understand more than: "*Prosze bardzo! Dziekuje!*" Well, she kept on receiving financial aid as long as it was available, I made sure of that.

I remember another case very vividly. This was a very fine lady who came from Lithuania. She said she was the wife of an ex-cabinet member and had had to flee. She had a teenage son who suffered from tuberculosis. She said it was a mild case and all her son needed was about half a year more in a sanitarium, that she had to pay for. When it was cured they could emigrate. For some reason this help was denied her recently and she begged me to reinstate it. I reassured her I was going to see to it that she get uninterrupted help. She was most thankful, so much so that I began to feel uncomfortable, but glad that this case had a good chance for a happy ending. At least I hope that was what happened to them.

When I went to my boss's office to have it okayed, he asked me what religion that woman had. I had no idea. He asked me to get the whole file for his reviewing. As I went to get it I was thinking of the strange request and concluded that perhaps some of my collegues voted money to people who had the same religion they had had. I had never thought of that before. I simply recommended aid when I felt it was badly needed. I prayed that this woman with her son had any kind of religion but what I had. When I handed over the file to Mr. L. he reviewed it in one instant, by looking at the religion. It was Catholic. What relief I felt. He signed it and returned it to me, smiling. From then on he signed anything I asked for without casting one glimpse at it.

More than half a year went by and during that time a so-called *Second Displaced Persons' Law* was issued by President Truman. According to that I became eligible to apply for a new emigration visa to the United States. The only requirement was to return to the American Zone in Germany and put in the application from there. So, I said good-bye to all and returned to Germany. I headed for Frankfurt a/M. and immediately reported to the United Nations' IRO Offices.

This time I had all the necessary papers and took care of all that was needed for starting the emigration procedure. When they found out that I had worked for them both in Paris and Rome, I was offered a job instantly. That was a good feeling and I happily wrote to both Ervin and the Rileys about this lucky turn of events. I also needed new papers from the Rileys, which they promptly sent, and the wheels that finally were to take me overseas were set in motion.

In Frankfurt a/M. I was in charge of the children and their emigration. Most of these youngsters were war orphans or misplaced and lost children. Others were out of wedlock, the result of the meeting of an unknown *GI* and a German Fräulein. These children also came from all over eastern and central Europe and beyond. But whatever their mother language would have been, they all spoke German now as they had lived in Germany in one or another camp. I just wish to single out one incident that touched my heart. One little five-year-old girl was brought up by nuns in a convent in Fulda, some eighty kilometers north of Frankfurt a/M. She was adopted by a Belgian family. My boss was going to pick her up and bring her to Frankfurt, so she could leave with the transport for Belgium. He thought it might be better if a woman went along with him, the child might be less frightened. So he asked me and off we went the short ride with the inevitable chauffeur. We rang the bell and out came a nun already expecting us. Little Helga, a pale, blond, blue-eyed, and sad-looking little girl was ready. She was nicely dressed in coat and cap, holding a small suitcase. She looked at us while she was holding on to one of the nuns for dear life; she would not let go. As we knew from her case history she had never known her parents or remembered any other place but this convent; it was her home, her only home. Finally one of the nuns ordered her to let go and join us. I took her hand, she let me, and we left with the car. She was quiet, she just looked somewhat bewildered. After a little while she came closer to me and called me "Mama." It almost broke my heart. Neither my boss, nor I dared say anything. Our voices would have betrayed our emotions. I hope you're happy, little Helga, and that you grew up into a fine woman and have your own family.

After several months I was transferred to Schweinfurt, where I had to spend a whole month under rigorous physical surveillance with thousands of other refugees. We had to be in tip-top shape to be able to emigrate to the New World, into a new life. I shared a spacious room with a mother and her two small children and a young girl. My companions were Poles again. We spoke to each other in German. The Polish woman was a very beautiful and shapely specimen. I had no idea where her husband was, if alive. Her son must have been six and the little girl four or five. There was an endless row of visitors who came to pick her up. Her children called them all "uncle."

One evening, after she put her children to bed, she approached me. I looked up, sensing something unusual. She chit-chatted a little, then she blurted out: "I have to tell you that I fell in love with the priest in our church. He's Hungarian. Do you know him?"

"No, I haven't met him," and I wondered why she told me about it.

"Do you think you could get acquainted with him, as he's your countryman and somehow let him know how I feel? Quite discreetly, of course," and she looked at me with those dreamy eyes of hers.

I found the request, no, the whole situation so comical that I told her, quite tongue in cheek, that I think she should go to the confessional and admit it herself. To my consternation she thanked me quite in earnest. I just about forgot about the whole thing when next Monday she came to me again. She looked positively radiant, when she told me this:

"I talked to the priest, who didn't seem to be surprised at all. I would say he seemed flattered. He thought my problem needed personal attention and counseling. He offered to help me if I met him in the evening." She stopped here and smiled happily, then continued to talk: "He knew of course that I was about to sail within that week. Since there was so little time we met every evening and I feel I'm on cloud nine. Agi, this priest also confessed to me that I was the only one and he'd follow me to Chicago at his earliest possible assignment."

As I lost contact with her I never found out the outcome of this unorthodox relationship.

The big day arrived and I found myself in Bremerhaven, boarding a navy boat, the *SS General Sturgis* that brought me to the U.S.A. The ten days we spent on the ship passed fast. I worked in the office to type endless lists as a volunteer worker and I also took walks on and off on the deck to stare at the immense Atlantic. It was calm weather all the way; only a sporadic choppiness rocked the ship occasionally. One day people spotted birds and soon the outline of the shore became clearer. The skyline of New York was overwhelming and the Statue of Liberty beckoned to us, welcoming.

Once off the ship and in New York City I had just enough time to call Ervin. I did this with the help of an escort who was at first reluctant to let me leave the group, lest I get lost. Finally she agreed and helped me to put the call through.

Ervin was ecstatic that I had finally made it. Since my train was about to leave very soon, there was no time for him to come and see me. He promised to visit me in Seattle as soon as it was possible.

It took almost four days of train-riding to cross this vast country. We transferred once, in Chicago. I was constantly looking out the window and marveling at the various countrysides.

On the fourth day the train rolled into the railroad station in Seattle. The Rileys were waiting for me with Rozsika. She spotted me almost as soon as I stepped off the train and ran towards me. I in turn hardly recognized her. She had become a lovely young lady, beautifully dressed with a fashionable hairdo. She hugged me and wouldn't let go. We all shed tears of happiness and I have to admit I felt almost like reaching home, so friendly and warm were the Rileys toward me. Rozsika must have painted a flattering picture of me.

Mr. Riley drove his car from the station all the way to their home that was on Lake Washington. The yard was manicured and Rozsika instantly showed me with great pride that she had a vegetable garden. They showed her how to grow all sorts of things. She also told me how they bought her a sled after they found out how her poor mother had promised her one but she never got it. Later on she learned to ski and was quite good at it, so the Rileys told me.

I noticed the strong resemblance between Rozsika and her father, just as I had imagined it. But in her eyes, though of a different shade, glowed the light of intellect she had inherited from her mother. If she could have seen her daughter!

Seattle was such a surprise. I couldn't get over its natural beauty. If we drove west or east, at the end of the horizon loomed the jagged mountain range of either the Olympics or the Cascade Mountains, almost hugging Seattle with their snowy peaks. Then to the south loomed Mt. Rainier in its pristine majesty. Evenings, after work followed by the family supper, I often took the rowboat—with their permission—and paddled out to the middle of the lake. There was no sound other than the little waves happily lapping on the side of the boat. An occasional quackle of the mallards swimming and fishing interrupted the peacefulness. One or two ducklings were sitting on the back of their mother comfortably and snugly. I almost envied them. Then, when I reached my favorite spot, I put the oars down and just sat there, almost hypnotized by the sight.

Mt. Rainier with its eternal snowcap often looked more like an apparition than a mountain firmly rooted on earth. Clouds settled at its bottom, seemingly making it look afloat, like a mirage. Its whiteness changed in the sunset, reflecting a wide gamut of pink, lavender, blue, and endless shades in between that have no name. It was fascinating. I never tired of gazing at it and it always filled me with awe and a deep peace.

Then there were the lakes in the midst of the city, with lovely homes and gardens. Camelias, azaleas, rhododendrons, and other flowers, whose names I only learned later on, beautified the whole landscape. Then there was Puget Sound, the bay of the Pacific Ocean.

I learned to smell, eat, and name seafood I was not familiar with before. The open markets were filled with all kind of iced creatures coming from an unknown world, the sea. I was taken to a so-called salmon fry on the sandy beaches. I also learned to dig for clams. I had to buy so called pedal-pushers to be appropriately dressed for such occasions. Mrs. Riley was most helpful and I believe she enjoyed coming with me to the various department stores to choose the best possible outfits. Now, there was an *embarras de richesse* if I ever saw one. Even Paris could pale next to it. I almost felt as if I had been transposed onto another planet—and it was only another continent. But what a continent!

The Rileys' home exuded comfort, well-being, and good taste. Not that I wasn't used to it, but it had been a long time and I had gone through a lot since I lost it. It was more than overwhelming to be in such an environment and to be accepted in one, even if it wasn't my own. My own, I thought. I sure yearned for a home of my own, for a life of my own to put all the horror behind me. Was Ervin the answer? I liked him and respected him, but I was not in love with him.

I had to concentrate on my new life now. I wanted to work and earn my living even if I had accepted the Rileys' hospitality for the time being. They wanted to send me to the University of Washington to study whatever I was interested in. I thanked them profusely, but I did not desire to have a career. I was hoping I would get work, interesting work for the time being. I went to an employment agency downtown. After having filled out the papers and after the lady looked at them, she made some calls and sent me to one of the large hospitals. I was familiar with medical terminology and had a good Latin background and some knowledge of Greek. These were helpful and I landed a job in the business office. I was billing King County and Blue Cross. I learned to do it fast and got a raise soon. I was very pleased with it. I rode the bus back and forth to work. It was time-consuming, as the distance was great, but very much worth while. But it was only five times a week. I liked to have such long weekends.

Ervin called regularly, but he kept putting off his visit. It was rather costly. I was sorry for this but I certainly understood. The distance was enormous between the two coasts.

Now that I had a regular life and excellent food, I started to develop headaches. I had never had headaches before. I didn't want to alarm the Rileys, but since I worked in a hospital I asked them to recommend a physician who wasn't very far either from the hospital or from the home, so I could have him look at me. I was given a name and address and I went to see him. By that time I had health insurance through my job. The doctor asked me a lot of questions, after all the tests came back negative. He spent a year's insurance money with the most complicated X-rays and lab tests. He looked at me and asked me point-blank if I believed in God.

I was stunned that he thought that my headaches were psychosomatic. All right, I thought, I went through a lot. Others suffered more, again others less. But most people got out and survived and went on with their lives without having gotten unbalanced or seriously affected mentally. I resented his suspicion although it might have come from genuine empathy. Nevertheless his judgment was misplaced. It took me a bit before I regained my calm and answered. "Yes, I do. I just lost my faith in Man."

If that satisfied him or not, I don't know. But I remembered that he had mentioned that he recently met a fellow physician from Hungary who had just started his practice here. He mentioned the name and I stored it in my memory. I was going to see him; I was hoping he'd be more helpful. I made the appointment over the phone. When I went to see him I told him the symptoms and also what the other doctor did. His first question was if a blood test and urine analysis had been made.

"No, but everything else was."

He just gaped at me. "What? Are you sure?"

Well, he took blood and went to the lab next to his office and did the test himself. While I was waiting I looked at the numerous photographs framed on the wall. They showed lakes, flowers, mountains very artistically "shot."

He came back and sat down behind his desk.

"You're extremely anemic, hence the headaches. Nothing else is wrong evidently. It must be due to malnutrition over a long period. Simply eating well will not suffice. I have to give you liver injections plus strong iron pills and in no time your headaches will be gone."

What a relief it was. I thanked him and made an appointment for the next injection. I had to go twice a week for a while. I told the Rileys about it and they offered to give me a ride, but I said I could make it easily after work. The doctor would wait for me. He was living in the same building where his office was. He understood that I was working and couldn't come during regular office hours.

My life became quite regular and it seemed quite natural to stay with the Rileys. I can't think of more affectionate people, more helpful and more kind-hearted. It was really a home for Rozsika and I felt rather happy there myself. I knew that I wasn't going to stay there forever but for the time being it was a wonderful solution and I felt completely at ease with them. They asked a lot, but always added, if I didn't wish to talk about it, they'd understand. So slowly they had a good clear picture of what my life was like before, during, and after the war. They were definitely three different lives.

They begged me to write it all down, but I explained that I wished to put it behind me and concentrate on making a new life for myself. "Perhaps," I added, "when I get old, I might just do that. I'm sure I shall never forget any part of it, good or bad. But just now I don't want to dwell on it anymore."

They didn't bring up the subject again. I think they understood and I was thankful for that.

XIII.

When I went for my next injection I heard beautiful music. It was most pleasant to wait in the sitting room for the doctor to call me.

"How lovely that you play the *Eroica*," I said before I even returned his greeting.

He smiled. "So, you know it?"

And thus started a conversation about music. It was followed by playing a Mozart sonata from the notes he had. I recognized the pale green Koehler edition from Europe. He played the fiddle and I accompanied on the piano. We had a wonderful time and I suddenly realized that it was rather late and the Rileys were going to worry about my whereabouts. So I called them. They thanked me that I thought of calling.

I dreamt that night that I was in my old home with my parents and we performed amidst our own circle, with a new face present, that of the doctor.

He liked to talk Hungarian to me; he said it was natural as long as I came from the same place and background. We found more things in common and pretty soon we spent all our free time together. I felt happy and quickly realized that I was in love. Emil, that was his first name, also expressed his feelings and we set the date for the wedding after half a year of acquaintance.

I wrote to Ervin about it, who called me and also wrote me a long letter. He was genuinely happy for me. He also admitted that he had found someone he planned to share the rest of his life with.

I hesitated a long time about whether to let Oskar's mother know. I brought it up with Ervin and Emil too. We talked it over from every angle and the verdict was finally that I would not. It would underline a finality, almost blotting out hope for her. Not as if I could influence fate, her son's fate by taking this step, still psychologically it would have been a blow to her.

In his long letter Ervin summed up his view on Oskar; the way he perceived an image I transmitted to him and he in turn analyzed it. He pointed out briefly that Oskar never knew any kind of privation in his life. He had it all and somehow he yearned for a fight, for difficulties to overcome, to make him feel that he had achieved something and not just sat down into the plush armchair prepared for him by his family. He needed self-confidence that he had it in him to struggle and get somewhere in life. Perhaps that was what made him seek out danger to such degree. Of course it was totally unselfish, heroic; after all, he risked his life all the time. But having lost it wouldn't have been such a blow to him as not finding his self-worth.

I pondered over that for a while and agreed with Ervin's opinion about Oskar. I also became very aware of Death reaching for you when and where Death decided, not unlike in the JOHN O'HARE story "Appointment in Samarra." In it the merchant's servant, having seen Death approach him in Bagdad, asked his master to go with him to Samarra, so Death wouldn't find him there. The master obliged and when they saw Death again, this time in the market place of Samarra, he accosted Him, asking why he had threatened his servant. Death answered that he did not, he was merely astonished to see him in Bagdad, as he had an appointment with him in Samarra.

Perhaps Oskar had an appointment with Him too somewhere, just like all those who perished in such cruel circumstances. Then I remembered something that Oskar had told me. He chose as his motto these words of Benjamin Franklin: "The highest worship of God is service to Man." Well, he served Man to the fullest of his capacity never minding the price he had to pay for it.

To return to the present:

We spent a wonderful weekend together: the Rileys, a few of their friends I had already met, Rozsika with her girlfriends, and finally Emil. We went for a picnic. We hiked, we sang, we laughed. It was all carefree and happy. All evil was behind me, locked up in the past.

When I went to my room that night, it was rather late. It was so quiet that I involuntarily almost tiptoed as I did not wish to intrude upon the stillness. I descended the two steps leading into that friendly room I occupied now. The windows were open. The chintz curtains matched the blue bedspread and the tiny white and deep pink flower pattern seemed to wink at me goodnaturedly. The batiste ruffles in front of the window moved ever so slightly in the light breeze coming from the lake. I sat down in the wooden rocking chair, which was also covered with pillows of that same blue pattern, and shut my eyes to drink in the peace that was a constant occupant. It was there before me and would surely stay there after me. It was an enchantment that was an organic part of that place. I opened my eyes again to take it all in. The moon shone bright, leaving a silvery bridge on the dark water that barely breathed in tiny splashes. All ducks and fowl were safely tucked in and were oblivious to it all. I went to the window and leaned on the inside sill. Nothing stirred. I got undressed in the dark and went to bed, still looking out as if mesmerized by the moon, the quiet lake. I must have been half asleep when I heard the barely audible strained sounds of a waltz. It *was the* waltz, our waltz with Oskar from so long ago. I mean the Oskar of the dodanella connection, from the turn of the century. Johann Strauss's *Der Waldmeister*. We danced to it the first time we met and it became our favorite. It has a slow rhythm, an elegant one, suiting Oskar to perfection. Any time that old life presented itself in my nightmare, or in my split memory, the waltz's lilting tune sounded faintly in the background.

My gosh, I thought, *not again!* I'm not going to have another of those nightmares. Poor Aunt Caroline wasn't anymore, and nobody gave me the dodanella tea to drink. What was going on? I thought I was all right, no more disturbances. *What would the Rileys think of me, and what about Emil? Please, let me just stay happy and don't complicate it all.* But I kept hearing the music, if nothing else presented itself. Was it possible that someone was really playing it? Was there a barge on the dark water and someone just happened to like it and wanted to listen to it? I was sure I was not the only one who liked it, even if I had some special memories and fear attached to it.

I have to admit I was not sure which was the case. But at least I had no nightmare go along with it this time, only rather pleasant old, old memories. *Oskar.* Would I meet him again? I don't mean in this life. I was thinking of a future life. Would he make my acquaintance again and would we fall in love again and would he vanish again? Three is a magic number; perhaps the third time I'd be able to hold on to him.

The lilting waltz echoed in my ears faintly and then slowly died away, while I went to sleep without having any dreams.

I woke up refreshed the next morning and was greatly relieved after the previous night's memory came back to me. I even hummed the tune as I washed myself and got dressed. Then I stopped short. Was I really humming that melody that had haunted me so frequently and that I feared so? I realized then with great relief that I was cured forever. It wouldn't haunt me anymore. I was free of the past at last. I fell in love again and not with Oskar. I felt like a reborn person.

Before I finish my story I would like to tell you about a wedding present that came in the form of a dream. It was the most precious gift I ever received and its memory will stay with me to the end of my days.

I saw an expense of silky lawn spreading over a low hill. There was a weeping willow tree and underneath it a chair. My father sat in this chair.

I somehow knew that this place was a cemetery, although there was no sign of tombstones. He was dressed in one of his gray suits with an impeccable shirt and handsome tie. His hair was brushed so every strand was in its place. He looked every bit the distinguished gentleman, the way I used to know him.

He did not speak to me, just looked at me with a hint of smile in his eyes. And his smiling eyes "told" me that he would always love me and he wished me all the happiness in the world.